habits

GILL HASSON

habits

How Small Changes

Make a Big Difference

Registered Office(s)
John Wiley & Sons, Inc., 111 River Street, Hoboken, NJ 07030, USA
John Wiley & Sons Ltd, New Era House, 8 Oldlands Way, Bognor Regis, West Sussex, PO22 9NQ, UK

For details of our global editorial offices, customer services, and more information about Wiley products visit us at www.wiley.com.

The manufacturer's authorized representative according to the EU General Product Safety Regulation is Wiley-VCH GmbH, Boschstr. 12, 69469 Weinheim, Germany, e-mail: Product_Safety@wiley.com.

Wiley also publishes its books in a variety of electronic formats and by print-on-demand. Some content that appears in standard print versions of this book may not be available in other formats.

Library of Congress Cataloging-in-Publication Data

Names: Hasson, Gill author
Title: Habits : how small changes make a big difference / Gill Hasson.
Description: Hoboken, NJ : John Wiley & Sons, Inc, 2026. | Includes index.
Identifiers: LCCN 2026004296 (print) | LCCN 2026004297 (ebook) | ISBN
  9781907326370 paperback | ISBN 9781907326394 adobe pdf | ISBN
  9781907326387 epub
Subjects: LCSH: Habit | Change (Psychology)
Classification: LCC BF335 .H36 2026 (print) | LCC BF335 (ebook)
LC record available at https://lccn.loc.gov/2026004296
LC ebook record available at https://lccn.loc.gov/2026004297

Cover Design: Wiley
Cover Image: © VVadi4ka/stock.adobe.com

Set in 11/14 pt and Sabon LT Std by Straive, Chennai, India
Printed and bound by CPI Group (UK) Ltd, Croydon, CR0 4YY

C9781907326370_130426

Contents

Contents

Introduction

Success doesn't come from what you do occasionally. It comes from what you do consistently.

—Marie Forleo

Maybe you've tried to start a good habit – like walking more or drinking water more often – a number of times and felt frustrated when it didn't stick. Perhaps you've tried breaking a bad habit – staying up too late, impulse spending online, or mindless scrolling on your phone – but, no matter how many times you tried, you failed to make the change last.

But as someone once said: 'Insanity is doing the same thing over and over again and expecting different results'.

If you've tried and failed to build a healthy habit or drop a bad habit more than once, it's time to try a different approach.

The reasons and excuses we give ourselves for stopping can sound convincing, yet they keep us stuck and make change feel impossible. But with the right strategy and support, establishing good lasting habits is absolutely possible. Breaking bad habits is entirely possible too.

Quite simply, you need to make good habits easier and bad habits harder. This book – *Habits* – will explain how.

Part One: *Understanding Habits and the Foundations of Change* begins by explaining what a habit is – its purpose, how a habit works, and what influences it – whether it's a simple habit like locking the back door each night, a healthy habit such as exercising daily, or an unhealthy habit like smoking or vaping.

Developing positive, helpful habits – and letting go of unhelpful ones – can make a big difference to your physical and mental health and wellbeing. In Chapter 2 you will read that physical and mental wellbeing are built through small daily habits that reinforce each other, with physical health supporting mental resilience and good mental health, making healthy routines easier to sustain.

A positive approach is crucial. A positive mindset is the foundation for building new habits – helping you begin from a place of confidence and optimism, rather than uncertainty and pressure. Having a positive outlook doesn't, though, mean ignoring or denying the challenges and difficulties, it means acknowledging them and then, rather than letting potential difficulties discourage or stall you, looking for helpful ways to move forward. Chapter 3 offers advice on starting habit change with this positive approach.

In Part Two: *The Practice of Habit Change: Turning Intentions into Action* we explore a range of ideas, approaches, and strategies to help you start and maintain a new good habit.

You'll learn that relying on willpower to start and maintain a new habit is a common mistake. Instead, the aim is to make the habit so easy that it requires little or no willpower, because the easier a habit is, the more likely it is to stick.

Just as you eat an elephant one bite at a time, the same is true for building a new habit. You take it one bite at a time. Chapter 4 explores the value of starting small – how a little effort at the beginning is enough to get started, build momentum, and make it easier to keep going – while Chapter 5 explains how linking new habits to existing routines and organising your environment can make them easier to maintain.

So far, so good. But what if your new habit is something you feel you *should* do, but don't really want to do, like exercising regularly or keeping up with household chores? You know it's important and that sticking with it will feel rewarding in the long run, yet you just can't seem to maintain it consistently. The answer is to make the habit both enjoyable and rewarding enough to do so that you *want* to do it. You can do this by pairing the task – something you *should* do – with something you *want* to do – something enjoyable. As well as pairing a new habit with something you enjoy doing, you can further increase your motivation if you give yourself a reward right after you complete it. Chapter 7 has ideas to help you to both enjoy a new habit and reward yourself for doing it.

Lasting habits aren't, though, just driven by rewards; they also depend on how well the behaviour reflects who you are or want to become. In Chapter 8 you'll learn about the concept of 'identity-based habits'. You'll discover that the more you perform a habit that aligns with how you see yourself and who you are becoming, the more you gain evidence that this identity is true – that this *is* what you do and this *is* who you are. You're then likely to feel motivated and encouraged to continue the habit, which creates a positive feedback loop that further reinforces the identity – the person you are becoming.

Chapter 8 further explains that your identity – who you are – and your habits are also shaped by the influence and support of other people. Other people's interest, support, and encouragement make new habits feel rewarding and create accountability. Their support can also help you recover from setbacks and get back on track.

By this point in the book you'll have a good understanding and a wealth of ideas, approaches, and strategies to inspire and motivate you.

However, it's important to know that meaningful change can take time. New habits don't become automatic overnight. Even when you've established a new habit, there's a chance you might slip up and revert back to your old way of thinking and behaving. You won't, though, have failed – setbacks are normal and to be expected. Chapter 9 offers guidance on how to handle difficulties, mistakes, and setbacks and get back on track.

Once a habit is formed, it becomes resistant to change, especially when the same cues, contexts, routines, rewards, and identity – your sense of 'who I am' – remain in place. This is good news for good habits and bad news for bad ones.

Just as when trying to build a good habit, when trying to change a bad habit we often rely on willpower and self-discipline, hoping determination alone will be enough. But again, relying on willpower and self-control is a mistake;

lasting change comes from making the bad habit harder to do and replacing it with a different one.

In Part Three: *Why Bad Habits Persist – and How to Change Them*, Chapter 10 explores how bad habits form, why they persist, and why they can be so difficult to break. It revisits the habit-formation theories introduced in Chapters 4–8, this time focusing on how those same principles apply to negative habits.

Chapter 11 explores a range of strategies for breaking bad habits, with a continued focus on a positive mindset, taking small manageable steps, shaping your environment, and the role of identity in lasting change.

As with good habits, bad habits don't disappear overnight. Even when you've established a change, there's a chance you might slip up and revert back to your old way of behaving. But you haven't failed – it's important to know that setbacks are normal and to be expected. Chapter 11 offers guidance on how to handle difficulties, mistakes, and setbacks and get back on track. Treating yourself with kindness and patience helps you reset more quickly and supports the positive identity you're on your way to achieving.

The final chapter of the book – Chapter 12 – explores the differences between habits and addictions, habits and OCD behaviours.

Habits, addictions, and OCD are all automatic behaviours. However, a habit is something that you can consciously control, while an addiction is a compulsive need that continues despite harmful consequences. When a behaviour causes serious harm to health, relationships, work, or finances, it is likely an addiction rather than a relatively harmless or annoying habit. OCD behaviours are repetitive actions that a person does in order to reduce intense anxiety caused by obsessions – intrusive, distressing thoughts or fears. Unlike habits, OCD behaviours are urgent, anxiety-driven, and hard to stop, temporarily relieving distress while reinforcing the obsession.

If you think you may have an addiction or OCD that is significantly affecting your life, it's important to seek help. Effective treatment and support are available, and this chapter includes information on where to find them.

Finally, included in the back of book are habit templates that you can use to help you plan the steps you can take to build a good habit and break a bad habit.

Note: AI was used to help create case studies and inform practical examples of ideas, theories, and concepts.

Understanding Habits and the Foundations of Change

1
What Is a Habit?

Habit is a cable; we weave a thread each day, and at last we cannot break it.

—Horace Mann

In her teenage years, Joelle was an avid reader of books, but now, in her 30s, she never seems to have the time. Recently, Joelle realised how much she missed the enjoyment of reading a good novel. She wanted to get back to reading so she decided to set her alarm just 20 minutes earlier each morning and read a few pages with a cup of coffee before doing anything else. The first couple of days she was tempted to ignore her alarm, but she didn't give in and, after two weeks, it became a routine which Joelle looked forward to. By the end of the year, Joelle had read and enjoyed 14 books. She felt more focused and relaxed each morning.

Every night after dinner, Tom told himself he'd just check his phone for a few minutes – scroll through messages, maybe watch a couple of videos. But a few minutes always turned into an hour or more. Before he knew it, Tom had spent the evening watching random clips and comparing his day to what other people had posted about their day. Finally, he would go to bed tired and annoyed with himself, telling himself that tomorrow night would be different. But it never was.

Leah used to be an early riser, starting each day with a run and a healthy breakfast. But after a few late nights at work, she hit the snooze button once, then again the next day, and again a few times the following week. Soon, morning runs disappeared, and breakfast became whatever she had time for before rushing out the door. What started as a small choice turned into a daily habit that left her feeling sluggish before the day had even begun. It wasn't until a friend asked, 'When's the last time you ran?' that Leah realised how far she'd drifted from the routine that made her feel good.

These three stories share a theme: each story shows that what we repeat – whether helpful or unhelpful – eventually becomes our default behaviour. It becomes a habit.

Joelle *built* a new habit (reading again) by repeating it daily until it became automatic. Tom *reinforced* a bad habit (evening phone use) through nightly repetition. Leah *lost* a good habit (morning runs) after a few small changes disrupted her routine.

Despite our best intentions, many of us struggle with dropping bad habits and establishing new, good habits. And yet at some time in our lives, we *have* each dropped a bad habit – staying up too late, for example, or smoking or vaping. And we all have good habits: the habit of looking both ways before crossing the street and the habit of brushing your teeth at the beginning and end of the day are habits that we have no problem carrying out.

Whether it's what you eat and drink, how much you exercise, the way you interact with others, how you structure your workday, or even how you think, developing positive, helpful habits – and letting go of unhelpful ones – can make a big difference to your physical and mental health and wellbeing.

To make those changes effectively, it helps to first understand what a habit is and how habits work.

A habit is simply a behaviour that's repeated regularly until it becomes automatic. Whether it's a healthy habit, like regular exercise, or a less helpful one, like snacking on sugary foods, most habits follow a habit loop – a learned connection between a cue (something that prompts the behaviour) and a response (the behaviour itself).

Habit loops

A habit loop is a concept from psychological and neuroscientific research explained by Charles Duhigg in his 2012 book *The Power of Habit*. In the book, he describes how habits form through a simple three-part cycle: cue → routine → reward.

Cue: Habits begin with cues that prompt automatic responses, even when we don't consciously notice them. A cue acts as a prompt that your brain learns to associate with a specific action. For example, feeling stressed (an internal cue) could prompt a habitual response – maybe to smoke a cigarette or to eat chocolate. Seeing your running shoes by the door (external cue) could be the cue for you to go for a run. Shutting the front door is the cue to lock it.

In the stories at the beginning of the chapter, Joelle's cue was her morning alarm and cup of coffee. Tom's cue was finishing dinner and seeing his phone on the table. Leah's cue was the sound of her alarm – but tiredness led her to hit snooze.

Routine (or behaviour): This is the action or behaviour that follows on from the cue. It's the habit itself – smoking a cigarette or eating chocolate or going for a run. The running shoes are the cue, going for the run is the routine or behaviour. Another example is the habit of looking both ways when you cross a road. The edge of the pavement and the intention to cross the road is the cue, looking both ways is the behaviour.

Joelle's routine – her habit – was reading her book, Tom's routine was scrolling through his phone and Leah's was hitting the snooze button and going back to sleep.

A cue can trigger different kinds of routines and behaviours – physical or mental – that make up the routine part of the loop. Physical behaviours are the observable actions – for example, having a snack (cued by an ad break while watching TV) or biting your nails (cued by feelings of anxiety).

Mental behaviours are thoughts and feelings prompted by a cue. For example, when you're reminded of someone who, a long time ago, you argued with and have not spoken to since, you replay the argument in your head.

Reward: The reward is the positive outcome your brain receives from completing the routine. It might be a feeling of achievement, satisfaction, relief, distraction, comfort, or relaxation. The habit of going for a run, for example, may be rewarded by a sense of achievement and feeling mentally and physically energised. The habit – the routine – of replaying the argument is rewarded with feelings of self-justification or righteousness.

Joelle's reading habit gave her pleasure and a sense of calm. Tom's scrolling habit rewarded him with entertainment. Leah's snooze habit gave her comfort and pleasure.

Rewards aren't always something you consciously notice. More often, they're felt subconsciously as emotional or physical relief, comfort, or pleasure. This reward is what reinforces the habit loop, teaching your brain to repeat the behaviour the next time the cue appears.

The habit loop: from cue to craving to reward

As you keep responding to the same cue, your brain begins to automate the behaviour. The cue–behaviour–reward loop becomes more efficient, requiring less conscious thought or effort. Over time, your brain even starts to *anticipate* the reward as soon as it detects the cue, which strengthens the habit and makes it feel automatic.

This subconscious learning is what cements the habit loop and keeps the behaviour firmly in place.

Duhigg views cravings as the driving force of the habit loop. They're what make a cue powerful, because the cue triggers a desire for the reward. That craving – often an emotional or mental urge, like wanting enjoyment, calm, relief, or a sense of control – compels you to carry out the routine so you can experience the reward. Once your brain recognises the cue, it immediately begins anticipating – and craving – the reward it has learned to expect.

So the cue sparks the craving, the craving drives the routine, and the routine delivers the reward. That reward then strengthens the connection, making it even more likely that the same cue will trigger the same behaviour the next time it appears.

The science

Rewards and dopamine
When a habit leads to a positive or pleasurable result, your brain releases dopamine – a chemical that signals reward and satisfaction. This release doesn't just make you feel good in the moment; it also strengthens the brain's connection to whatever behaviour caused it. In other words, dopamine motivates you to repeat that action again, because your brain now associates it with pleasure and a sense of wellbeing.

Neural pathways
The core components of the brain are neurons: cells in the nervous system that process and transmit information. The interconnections between neurons mean that when you do or think in a new way your brain creates new connections – neural pathways. It's like when you walk through a field of long grass, each step helping to create a new path. If you then regularly walked that same path through the field of long grass, very soon you would make a clearly defined path that you would take each time you wanted to cross that field. You wouldn't think about it, you'd just automatically take that path.

In the same way, when you repeat a behaviour or thought, your brain continues using the same neural pathway and so it becomes stronger and deeper.

Over time, this forms a habitual pathway that your brain can follow with little effort. That's why repeated behaviours can become automatic: the brain is simply following a well-worn path.

Using a weekly habit as an example, here's how neural pathways and dopamine work together in habit formation.

1. A cue (end of the week, Friday evening) activates the neural pathway linked to the behaviour or habit (order a takeaway meal).
2. You perform the behaviour or habit (order the takeaway and eat it).
3. You experience the reward (the meal, enjoyment, feeling full) dopamine is released, reinforcing the pathway that led to the reward.

Each repetition strengthens the pathway, making the habit more automatic and less dependent on conscious decision-making. (It's Friday evening, I'll order a takeaway.)

The cue–routine–reward loop can apply equally to internal emotional rewards (enjoyment, comfort, relief) or physical, external ones – something you can see, touch, or measure (food, money, etc.).

Pepsodent and the habit loop

In the early 1900s, few people in the US brushed their teeth regularly. Toothpaste wasn't a popular product and sales were low. That is until advertising executive Claude C. Hopkins was hired to market a new toothpaste called Pepsodent.

(*Continued*)

Hopkins recognised that people weren't interested in the prevention of future tooth decay; they wanted immediate benefits. So, he introduced the concept of 'the film' – a layer on teeth that was unsightly and could cause tooth decay and other dental problems. His adverts asked people to do the 'tongue test' – to run their tongue over their teeth and feel the 'film' for themselves, making the problem tangible and personal.

The advertising for Pepsodent explained how the toothpaste removed this 'film' – it cleaned your teeth and led to a more appealing smile.

Pepsodent included citric acid and mint oil, which created a cool, tingling sensation. That tingle became the reward – people associated the tingling with having clean teeth and saw it as proof that the toothpaste was 'working'. Furthermore, they started to miss it when they hadn't brushed, creating a craving and making brushing an essential daily habit.

Within a decade, daily toothbrushing in the US went from something few people did, to being a widespread habit; and by the 1930s, toothbrushing was a national norm.

Hopkins had created a *habit loop*.

Cue: The feel of the 'film' (plaque) on your teeth.

Routine: Brush with Pepsodent.

Reward: Tingling freshness and teeth feeling clean.

Today, toothbrushing is an automatic behaviour that most of us do twice a day without thinking about it.

Context: time, place, and circumstances

Charles Duhigg's habit loop suggests that cravings and rewards drive the formation of habits. However, not all habits are motivated solely by rewards. Often, context – the set of circumstances or facts that surround a particular event or situation – play a key role.

As a result of studies she conducted while at Northern California's Duke University, behavioural scientist Professor Wendy Wood suggests that many of our habits are the result of 'stable environments'. ('A New Look at Habits and the Habit-Goal Interface'. *Psychological Review*, 2007.)

Once a habit is formed, we often continue it without thinking or even noticing the outcome. The habit becomes automatic, requiring little or no motivation or conscious reward. The habit is just something you always do, without thinking about it at a particular time or when you're in a particular place. The habit of brushing your teeth each morning and evening happens – is cued – not so much for the expected reward but because you're in the bathroom (the place) first thing in the morning and last thing at night (the time). Another example is when you leave the house: shutting the front door and locking it. It's so automatic that later in the day it's easy to forget whether you did actually lock the door after shutting it.

And in another example, you might have a habit of buying a coffee at the same cafe on your way to work each morning. It started as a small daily treat – the coffee is good and the baristas are friendly. Eventually, your brain doesn't need the conscious reward anymore: the context alone – the time of day and the fact that it's on your usual route to work – triggers the habit.

The more frequently a behaviour is performed in a specific context, the stronger the mental association becomes, making the behaviour more likely to occur automatically in that context.

Wendy Wood's and Charles Duhigg's theories on habits share several key similarities, even though they differ in emphasis. They both agree that habits are automatic actions that require little to no conscious thought. They agree that performing the same behaviour repeatedly is necessary for habit formation and both agree that a consistent cue – whether internal (e.g., stress or boredom) or external (e.g., time and place) – is what initiates a habit.

But Charles Duhigg's habit loop focuses on what drives the habit – cue, habit, and reward – while Wood focuses on how stable environmental cues – time, place, circumstances – make a habit automatic.

Shopping habits

The layout of shops is often designed to prompt and reinforce shopper habits, using the same cue–routine–reward principles and contextual behaviours that influence habitual behaviour.

Familiar store layouts and aisle categories in supermarkets ('Ready Meals', 'Crisps & Savoury Snacks', 'Canned Vegetables & Fruit', etc.) make it easy for you to move through the store on autopilot.

If you shop regularly at a particular supermarket, you probably have a route you follow every time you enter. In each aisle, you know exactly where to find the items and products you usually buy. The experience becomes a reward loop; cue (enter store) – routine (shop along familiar route) – reward (the food items you buy).

Personal identity

Cues, cravings, rewards, and context – time, place, and circumstances – aren't the only things that shape our habits. Our habits are also influenced by our identity (who we are or want to become) and our values (what matters most to us and what we care about).

If, for example, you see yourself as someone who keeps fit and healthy, all your actions and behaviour reflect that identity – you're more likely to have habits that confirm it: healthy eating habits, physical fitness, and exercise habits.

Myra's healthy habits

Twice a week, before work, Myra goes out for a short run – not because she feels she should, but because it's just part of who she is. Seeing herself as 'someone who keeps fit and healthy' is reflected in her everyday choices. As well as running before work twice a week, Myra walks the one-mile distance to work and back home each day and she takes part in the five km Park Run each Saturday. She eats healthy, well-balanced meals but she's not obsessive about what she does and doesn't eat – she also enjoys pizza and chips and frequent lazy Sundays. And if she occasionally misses a run, she doesn't feel guilty. In the main, her habits consistently reflect who she is.

When a habit becomes something that reflects who you are rather than just what you do, it is likely to stick.

Conserving mental energy

Along with cues, cravings, rewards, and factors like time, place, and identity, habits also establish themselves because of the advantages that come from their automatic nature.

At first, a new behaviour or habit takes a lot of mental effort because it requires conscious thought – deciding, reasoning, planning, and remembering. But each time you repeat the new habit your brain strengthens the neural pathways that make the behaviour faster and more efficient. Over time, your brain needs to make less of an effort – you don't have to consciously think about what you're doing – the habit becomes automatic and frees up your mind to focus on other, unrelated things.

For example, when your brain doesn't have to consciously think about your morning routine – brushing your teeth, getting dressed, making coffee, getting breakfast, etc. – it frees up your brain for other things: thinking about and planning the rest of your day.

And in another example, when you are learning to drive, you need to pay close attention to many things at once: the road, traffic signals, other vehicles, steering, changing gear, and so on. This requires a significant amount of concentration.

However, with practice, driving becomes more automatic. You can talk to a passenger, listen to music, and drive without constantly thinking about every move – looking in the mirror, signalling, changing gear, etc. This is because the actions involved in driving have become automatic – habitual – requiring less conscious thinking.

Obama's routine

Habits make daily life more efficient by being automatic. In an interview in 2012, President Obama told the magazine *Vanity Fair* 'You'll see I wear only grey or blue suits. I'm trying to pare down decisions. I don't want to make decisions about what I'm eating or wearing because I have too many other decisions to make'.

It wasn't just what he wore each day that Obama routinised. Important issues requiring a decision from the President were submitted in writing (known as 'decision memos') with three check-boxes at the bottom: 'agree', 'disagree', and 'let's discuss'. 'You need', he said in the interview, 'to focus your decision-making energy. You need to routinise yourself'.

Key points

Habit loops

- A habit is simply a behaviour that's repeated regularly until it becomes automatic.
- In his 2012 book, *The Power of Habit*, Charles Duhigg explains how habits form through a simple three-part cycle: cue → routine → reward.

- The cue triggers an automatic response, the routine is the behaviour itself, and the reward is the positive outcome your brain receives from completing it.
- Rewards are often subconscious, experienced as emotional or physical relief, comfort, or pleasure. Rewards reinforce the habit loop, teaching your brain to repeat the behaviour the next time the cue appears.
- Over time, the cue–behaviour–reward loop becomes more efficient and automatic, with the brain anticipating the reward as soon as it detects the cue. The cue sparks a craving that drives the behaviour or routine, delivers the reward, and strengthens the connection so the same behaviour is more likely to occur again in the future.
- Over repeated cycles, the habit loop (cue → routine → reward) becomes faster and more automatic because the neural pathway is well established. Dopamine plays a role too: the brain anticipates the dopamine reward as soon as it detects the cue.

Context: time, place, and circumstances

- Not all habits are motivated solely by rewards. Professor Wendy Wood's studies suggest that for many habits, context – time, place, and circumstances – plays a key role.
- Once established, a habit becomes automatic and no longer requires conscious motivation or reward. A coffee-buying habit, for example, may begin as a small daily treat, but over time the context alone – such as the time of day and the cafe's place on your usual route to work – becomes enough to trigger it. Repeating a behaviour in the same context strengthens the mental association, making the habit increasingly automatic.

- Wendy Wood and Charles Duhigg both agree that habits are automatic actions formed through repeated behaviour and triggered by consistent cues. However, Duhigg's habit loop focuses on what drives habits – cue, routine, and reward – while Wood emphasises how stable environmental cues – such as time, place, and circumstances – make habits automatic.

Identity

- Habits are further influenced by our identity (who we are or want to become) and our values (what matters most to us and what we care about). If, for example, you see yourself as someone who keeps fit and healthy, you're more likely to have habits that reflect and confirm that identity.
- In turn, when a new, repeated behaviour starts to feel like who you are or who you are becoming, it's likely to turn into an established habit.

Conserving mental energy

- Habits also establish themselves because of the advantages that come from their automatic nature.
- At first, a new behaviour takes significant mental effort because it requires conscious decision, reasoning, planning, and remembering. With repetition, the behaviour becomes faster and more efficient – it becomes automatic – and so frees your mind to focus on other things.

2
Strong Foundations for Health and Wellbeing

There is no influence like the influence of habit.
—Gilbert Parker

Good habits play an essential role in supporting our physical and mental health and overall wellbeing. Our wellbeing – our ability to enjoy life and cope with its challenges without becoming overly stressed – is grounded in several areas of life: physical health, emotional balance, mental resilience, social and spiritual connection.

When it comes to good habits, creating lasting change becomes much easier when we focus on building a strong foundation for other positive habits to grow from. In other words, we need foundational habits.

Foundational habits are behaviours or routines that, once established, have a positive effect across other parts of your life. These habits form the base that supports overall wellbeing and make it easier to develop and sustain additional healthy behaviours.

Foundational habits – regular physical exercise, a balanced diet, and good quality sleep – anchor your routines, making life more structured and manageable. They don't just stand alone; they are part of a dynamic, each one affecting and supporting the others. A healthy diet, for example, provides energy for physical exercise and supports your body to repair from physical stress and strain. A balanced diet also supports emotional stability, as blood sugar swings can affect your mood. Regular exercise can improve sleep quality and eating habits. Each foundational habit actively supports and shapes another – often in a continuous, evolving way.

Physical and mental health

Mental and physical health habits work in a positive cycle – healthy habits support your wellbeing, and improved wellbeing makes it easier to sustain those habits and develop new ones. For example, regular exercise, healthy eating, and good sleep are habits that lead to better health. In turn, when you feel physically and mentally well, you have more energy, focus, and feel more inclined to maintain those positive habits.

So, good health and wellbeing work in both directions – they're the foundations that help good habits thrive, and there is benefit that comes from keeping those habits.

Physical health functions as a foundational habit because it supports and sustains many other habits and areas of your life.

Our physical health and mental health are closely linked; physical activity can be beneficial for your mental health and wellbeing too. The benefits can be immediate. When you're physically active, your brain releases endorphins – the 'feel good' hormones – which if you're troubled in some way, can calm you, reduce feelings of anxiety and stress, and lift your mood. Physical activity helps to break up racing or intrusive thoughts; being physically active can give your brain something other than your worries to focus on, leaving you less stressed and calmer.

Mental health and wellbeing are concerned with how we think, feel, and perceive the world – how our thoughts and feelings affect our actions and behaviour. Good mental health allows you to manage and adapt to a range of emotions and situations in a positive, constructive way.

The foundational habits that support your physical health – regular good quality sleep, balanced diet, and physical exercise – also support your mental health and provide stability, balance, and resilience for your mind.

When mental health is strong, it supports your ability to develop and maintain habits related to exercise, healthy eating, rest and sleep, social connections, and your ability to plan and organise your life. When your mental health is weakened – as a result of, for example, stress, anxiety, or depression – it becomes harder to maintain good habits. Even basic behaviours like eating well or getting rest can be a struggle.

Physical health habits

Our physical and mental health and wellbeing are nurtured through consistent, positive daily practices: small, repeated actions that become automatic over time. In other words, our health and wellbeing are sustained by habits. Below are examples of habits that support physical health.

Nutrition and hydration

- Eating balanced meals with plenty of fruit, vegetables, and whole grains.
- Drinking enough water throughout the day.

Exercise and movement

- Regular physical activity – walking, running, cycling, swimming, yoga, gardening, and housework.
- Regular strength training.
- Active movement in your daily routine – taking the stairs, walking or cycling instead of driving short journeys.
- Moving around every hour or so when sitting for long periods. Choosing active breaks over sitting for long periods.

Sleep

- Getting enough sleep.
- Maintaining a consistent sleep routine – going to bed and waking up at consistent times.

These foundational habits – sleep, physical movement, nourishment, hydration, and sleep – create a foundation for good physical health.

Mental health habits

Good mental health habits don't just manage and reduce stress, they provide you with a foundation for emotional stability, confidence, and a sense of control over your life. Good mental health habits help you enjoy life, manage challenges, and maintain resilience. Below are examples of habits that support mental health.

Positive social connections

- Spending time with friends and family members you enjoy being with – sharing mutual interests, experiences, and support. Regular check-ins by phone or messaging.
- Contributing to others, showing gratitude, showing compassion.

Time management

- Planning your day the night before by writing down your top three priorities. Then, focus on the three most important tasks.
- Using the two-minute rule: if something takes less than two minutes, do it immediately.
- Work/study habits: rather than multi-tasking, focus on one task at a time.
- Having boundaries: saying 'no' more often to other people's requests and demands.

Rest and relaxation

- Regular physical activity.
- Mindful activities – yoga, meditation.
- Engaging in creative activities, such as music, art, crafting, writing, cooking.
- Healthy boundaries and balance: maintaining limits on screen time and work hours.
- Small acts of self-care.
- Spiritual practice: activities and experiences that give you a sense of being part of and belonging to something bigger and more everlasting than yourself – a religion, a music festival, being a sports fan and spectator, being in nature, etc.

- Reading, journaling, listening to music, playing games, watching TV and films.
- Being out in nature.
- Having hobbies and interests.
- Learning and practising new skills – for example, a musical instrument or a foreign language.

By focusing on just one or two foundational habits to begin with, you create a strong base that makes positive, lasting change in other areas of your life much easier.

Keep track of your current patterns for a week. Think about your physical and mental health and wellbeing; is there one area in particular – sleep, healthier eating, physical activity and exercise, social connection, time management, rest and relaxation – that clearly needs addressing?

Whatever the area, that's where to start.

Key points

- Our physical and mental wellbeing are supported by small, positive daily actions that, through repetition, become habits.
- Mental and physical health habits reinforce each other: physical health habits improve mental wellbeing, and improved mental wellbeing makes physical health habits easier to maintain and build.
- Physical health habits – regular exercise, a balanced diet, adequate hydration, and quality sleep – support mental health by providing stability, balance, and resilience.

- Good mental health makes it easier to maintain everyday habits like exercise, healthy eating, sleep, rest, social connection, and time management, while also supporting emotional stability, confidence, resilience, and a sense of control over your life.
- By focusing on just one or two foundational habits to begin with, you create a strong base that makes further good habits easier to initiate and maintain.
- Track your current patterns for a week, identify the area of physical or mental wellbeing that needs the most attention and start there.

3
Making Change Feel Possible

If you believe you can change – if you make it a habit – the change becomes real.

—Charles Duhigg

Ty's all or nothing fitness plan

When Ty was at university, he belonged to the university gym and took part in weight training twice a week. He also played in the university's five-a-side football team. But over the following few years his fitness declined, so one New Year's Eve Ty decided he was going to get fit. Fired up with motivation, he decided to go to the gym three days a week after work and do an hour of weight training plus cardio each time.

For the first two weeks, Ty went to the gym every other weekday. But at the end of each session he felt wiped out. The next week he managed to go only twice and – by the following week – work deadlines and a family issue got in the way and Ty didn't go to the gym at all. He went once the week after that, but by the middle of February he'd given up entirely.

What went wrong? Quite simply, going from no exercise to three intense sessions a week was unrealistic. Ty was relying on willpower and self-control. There was nothing in his approach that helped make it easier for him to keep to his New Year resolution.

What's the problem?

Maybe, like Ty, you've had good intentions – to improve yourself or your situation in some way. Maybe you want to eat more healthily, drink more water or lose weight, get fitter or sleep better? Perhaps you've resolved to be more productive, meet up with friends and family more often. It could be that you've decided to learn something new, maybe a language or a musical instrument? But despite your good intentions, either you didn't get started or, after a few days or weeks, you failed to maintain your new good habit. And then you berated yourself for your inability to make your good intentions stick.

People often find ways to justify dropping or avoiding a new habit. Which of these reasons sound familiar to you?

- I don't have the time/energy/resources.
- The habit feels like one more thing I have to find time for.
- Life gets in the way – work deadlines or family responsibilities.
- I don't see results fast enough. I don't know if it's working.
- I lose motivation. When I come across difficulties I give up.
- The new habit is repetitive and boring.
- The new habit doesn't feel like me.
- I don't know how to do it. It's too difficult.

- I don't have much confidence in my abilities – I don't think I'm capable of achieving much.
- I started the habit, but I missed a few days – I've already blown it, so why bother?
- Temptations (junk food in the house, phone by the bed, no clear workspace) make the habit hard to stick to.
- I don't get help and support from other people.

These reasons can sound so convincing that they keep you stuck, making it feel like change is out of reach. But you're not weak, lazy, or lacking willpower – you simply need a new approach. With the right strategy and supports in place you absolutely can make it work – you can start a habit and make it stick.

In fact, like everyone else, you *have* already started and sustained good habits in your life. Think back to a time when you committed to something – maybe taking driving lessons, showing up for the five km Park Run every Saturday, learning a language, practising a musical instrument, or some other activity. It probably wasn't easy, but you kept at it. You created a habit of turning up for lessons, showing up at the park, or practising regularly and over time, it stuck.

You probably didn't stop to reflect on the strategies, the commitment, and the mindset that carried you through. But the fact remains – you did it once, and you can do it again. This book will help you uncover exactly what made those habits work – the approaches, the methods, and the mindset – so you can tap into that same ability whenever you want to introduce new, positive habits in your life.

Having a positive mindset

> Winners make a habit of manufacturing their own positive expectations in advance of the event.
>
> —Brian Tracy

When it comes to starting a new habit, the way you think – your attitude and approach – makes all the difference. You need a positive mindset. The following three steps can help.

Identify what you will gain. The first step towards a positive mindset is to keep in mind the good reasons to start the new habit. Why is it so important to you? What do you have to gain – in what way will you benefit? Maybe you'll be healthier, happier, or wiser. Perhaps you'll learn a new skill, or improve yourself or your situation in some way. Whatever it is, keep it in mind. Better still, write it down and place it somewhere you'll see it every day, or set it as your phone's screensaver as a regular reminder of why the change matters to you, what you have to gain, and how it connects to the person you want to become.

Imagine it. Visualise yourself doing the habit and feeling good while doing it. See yourself as someone for whom the habit is a normal part of your daily life.

Expect mistakes. Before you begin, remind yourself that there will be days when you slip up and that this is completely normal. (More about this in Chapter 9.) A positive mindset helps you stay open to learning, make adjustments, and be persistent enough to keep going.

A positive mindset helps you:

- have confidence in your ability to change: if you tell yourself 'I can do this', you're more likely to take the first step and stick with it;
- be willing to experiment: a positive approach and an open mind encourage you to try different strategies until you find what works for *you*;
- adapt to life's changes: if your routines, energy levels, and circumstances change, a positive approach encourages you to adapt your habits rather than abandon them altogether;
- accept setbacks: instead of seeing slip-ups as failures, you understand that mistakes are part of the process and you treat them as something to learn from; you adjust your approach and keep moving forward;
- be kind to yourself: if you do have a setback, instead of berating yourself, a positive mindset helps you encourage yourself in the same way you'd support a friend, making it easier to try again;
- focus on progress, not perfection: you acknowledge small wins; you recognise that even the smallest of wins counts.

A positive mindset is the foundation for building new habits – helping you begin from a place of confidence and optimism, rather than uncertainty and pressure.

Ravi, for example, struggled with healthy eating. Instead of focusing on the need to 'stop eating rubbish', he told himself he was aiming to make healthier food choices, acknowledging each and every small choice – like adding fruit to breakfast. This positive approach helped him build momentum and consistency.

And in another example, for Lin, study time had always felt like a chore until she started viewing it as an investment in her future. This shift in her approach helped her develop a sustainable learning routine.

Ravi and Lin's approaches both show how a positive mindset transforms new habits from something difficult and demanding into something positive and meaningful, making the habit easier to start, stick with, and grow.

Having a positive outlook doesn't mean denying the challenges and difficulties of a situation. Rather, you acknowledge the difficulties and challenges and then, rather than let them discourage or stall you, you look to engage with helpful ways to move forward.

The fresh start effect

Of course, a new habit can be started at any time, but research shows that 'temporal landmarks' do give you a motivational advantage, making it more likely you'll follow through.

In 2011, Professor Katy Milkman and her colleagues conducted a study, later published in 2014 in the journal *Management Science*, on what they called 'behaviour change interventions' – the deliberate actions people take to improve their behaviour. The study explored what is known as the 'fresh start effect'. It found that people are more likely to begin new habits, such as dieting or exercising, immediately after a temporal landmark – a meaningful date that marks a new beginning: the start of the week, month, or year, a birthday, or returning from a holiday.

It would appear that these moments can act as a mental reset button, creating a psychological separation between your 'old self' and your 'new self'. The separation between the two states helps you feel like you're starting from a clean slate – which increases motivation.

Temporal landmarks don't guarantee success but they do create the emotional momentum that makes starting a change in behaviour feel more meaningful.

You can use the 'fresh start effect' to your advantage – to kick-start your motivation. Set a start date for a new habit around a temporal landmark. Focus on the 'new you': if you do slip up for some reason, don't see it as having failed – don't berate yourself. Instead, see it a mistake made by the 'old you' and move back to the path the 'new you' is taking.

Key points

Reframing habit change

* Most likely, at some point in the past, you've had good intentions to improve yourself or your situation in some way – but struggled to start or maintain your new habit.

- The reasons and excuses we give ourselves for avoiding or dropping a good habit may sound convincing, but they keep us stuck, making it feel like positive change isn't possible.
- You have, though, successfully started and maintained a good habit before. You may not have paused to consider the mindset, strategies, and supports that got you there, but the fact remains – you've done it before, which means you can do it again.

Having a positive mindset

- A positive mindset is the foundation for building new habits – helping you begin from a place of confidence and optimism, rather than uncertainty and pressure.
- Having a positive outlook doesn't mean ignoring or denying the challenges and difficulties, it means acknowledging them and then, rather than letting them discourage or stall you, you look for helpful ways to move forward.
- Start by identifying why the new habit is important to you and how you will benefit. Then visualise yourself performing the habit and enjoying it.
- Expect mistakes – be kind to yourself – remind yourself that slipping up occasionally is normal and part of the process.

The fresh start effect

- You can use the 'fresh start effect' to kick-start a new habit by beginning at a temporal landmark, such as the start of a week, month, or year, a birthday, an anniversary, or after returning from a holiday.
- Focus on the 'new you'. If you do slip up, don't berate yourself. See it as a mistake made by the 'old you' and return to the path the 'new you' is taking.

PART TWO

The Practice of Habit Change: Turning Intentions into Action

4
Start Small to Grow Big

We are what we repeatedly do. Excellence, then, is not an act, but a habit.

—Aristotle

Once you've identified a reason to start a new habit, you have motivation – a purpose that gets you started. Motivation gives you direction and inspires you to begin new habits. If, though, motivation fades – when you're tired, stressed, or discouraged – you then have to rely on your willpower. You might, for example, not feel like going for a run but, somehow, you make yourself go. Willpower gives you the self-control to do something and keep going when you don't feel motivated.

But willpower is difficult to maintain – it requires effort, focus, and self-discipline, especially when you're stressed or tired.

According to several studies, we all have a limited amount of willpower and it's easily used up. When you have to exercise willpower and self-control in one situation, there's less willpower available to you for other situations, even if those situations are totally different from each other.

Spend some time reluctantly writing a report or putting together a presentation, and even though you intended to go clean the bathroom afterwards, or start filling in your tax return, your brain doesn't have enough energy left to motivate you. You've used up your willpower and fallen victim to 'can't power'.

It's a mistake to rely on willpower to make a habit stick. Instead, you'll need to make the habit so easy it requires little or no willpower at all. The easier a habit is, the higher the chances that you'll adopt it. So you have to make it easier for yourself.

Eating the frog

The American writer Mark Twain suggested that: 'If it's your job to eat a frog, it's best to do it first thing in the morning. And if it's your job to eat two frogs, it's best to eat the biggest one first'. The frog is that one thing you can't face doing and that you're most likely to put off. 'Eating the frog' means that you tackle the hardest, most unpleasant task first to build momentum for the rest of the day. The idea is that once you've done the most challenging task, everything else you plan on doing the rest of the day will feel easier.

But when it comes to starting a new habit, the suggestion that you start big isn't helpful. Habits need to start small otherwise they're unlikely to get off the ground. Instead of 'eating the frog', it's better to think in terms of planting a seed. You start small.

Saskia's small step fitness habit

In the last chapter, you'll have read about Ty's attempt to initiate a health and fitness habit. Like Ty, Saskia also wanted to get fitter. But unlike Ty, she chose the smallest, most doable step: to walk for 10 minutes after lunch, three times a week. That was it. No gym membership, no ambitious aims.

At first, the walks felt easy. She enjoyed the fresh air – even when it was raining – and found herself walking a little longer. After a few weeks, her 10-minute strolls turned into 20-minute brisk walks. She listened to music or podcasts to make them even more enjoyable and provide an immediate reward. It wasn't a big deal – she didn't have to announce a change. Saskia simply let the habit develop naturally, building confidence and momentum.

Ty's attempt failed because he tried to do too much, too soon. He overloaded himself and couldn't keep it up. Going from no exercise to three intense sessions a week was unrealistic. Ty was relying on willpower and self-control. There was nothing in his approach that helped make it easier for him to keep to his New Year resolution.

Saskia, on the other hand, succeeded because she kept her goal small and manageable – so simple she couldn't fail. Her story shows how starting small, then building consistency, is what is more likely to lead to lasting change. Starting with an easy win builds momentum and confidence – making further changes feel more achievable.

Choosing a direction: The first step to real change

In Chapter 2 you were asked to decide what area of your life you could identify as being the most out of balance right now. Maybe it was food and nutrition, or physical activity and exercise? Social connection? Time management, or sleep, rest, and relaxation? Something else?

In Lewis Carroll's book *Alice in Wonderland*, Alice has the following conversation with the Cheshire Cat.

Alice:	Would you tell me, please, which way I ought to go from here?
The Cheshire Cat:	That depends a good deal on where you want to get to.
Alice:	I don't much care where.
The Cheshire Cat:	Then it doesn't much matter which way you go.
Alice:	. . . So long as I get somewhere.
The Cheshire Cat:	Oh, you're sure to do that, if only you walk long enough.

This exchange illustrates why vague intentions don't produce meaningful change.

Alice wants to 'go somewhere', but she hasn't decided *where*. Because there's no destination, any direction seems acceptable and none is better than another. The Cheshire Cat points out the consequence: movement without direction guarantees motion, but not progress.

When it comes to starting a new habit if, like Alice, you don't know what you want, if you don't have a clearly defined habit to start with, you could well end up just about anywhere. And you could spend a long time getting there!

Whatever the area of your life you'd like to improve, like Alice you will need to think what direction you're going in and what your first specific step will be.

Start small to grow big

What would be an easy win for you? What would be a small habit you could start today? If you want to improve your health, it might be to drink a glass of water after breakfast, to add a vegetable to dinner every night, or to take a 10-minute walk after lunch each day. You could walk up the stairs at work rather than take the lift. Or park your car 10 minutes from your destination and walk the rest of the way.

Perhaps you want to be more organised at home. If you don't do this already, you could commit to making your bed every morning. Or wash the dishes immediately after every meal.

Or you might feel that starting with a habit that supports your mental and emotional health – for example, each evening, reflecting on and writing down three positive things that happened that day – is something you could definitely do.

If you want to get into a habit of saving money, rather than commit to a sum that's unrealistic, you might, for example, stop buying a coffee on your way to work each day and at the end of each week, transfer the money saved into a savings account.

If you're currently someone who struggles to take a lunch break, or eats at their desk, start by committing yourself to one or two days a week of taking your full lunch break away from your desk. Or make it even smaller – just take 20 minutes lunch break once or twice a week.

New habits need to be small and manageable enough to be consistently practised daily, helping you build momentum and a sense of achievement.

Here's some more examples of small shifts and how they add up to big change.

- Getting off the tube train or bus one stop earlier and walking the rest of the way. This can add thousands of steps per week.
- Each evening, writing down three small positive things that happened during the day (for example, that the sun was shining, you received a humorous message from a friend, you read a good book). Doing so helps develop a stronger and more positive mindset in just a few weeks.
- Listening to a podcast or audiobook during your commute. This turns into hundreds of hours of learning each year.
- Swapping two meat-based meals a week for a vegetarian option. Doing so could save you money, improve your health, and lower your environmental footprint.

- Practising focused breathing for two minutes daily. This gradually helps you lower your stress response and increase emotional resilience.
- Standing up and moving around once every hour at work. Small, frequent movements have measurable benefits – they reduce stiffness in joints and muscles, improve circulation, posture, and mobility. Regular movement helps counter some of the risks linked to prolonged sitting, such as cardiovascular disease, type 2 diabetes, and weight gain.
- Drinking a glass of water before every meal. This improves hydration and helps regulate appetite.
- Regularly sending a message to a friend or family member once a week – such as a photo, an observation, or a link to an article, podcast, or video you know they'd enjoy, or just to ask how they're doing. Over time, these small actions strengthen and maintain social connections and support networks.
- Saving a small amount each week for an emergency fund. This helps prevent relying on credit when something unexpected needs to be paid for.

Fran's story – slowly building calm

Fran wanted to feel less anxious. She'd read that meditation can have grounding, calming effects, so she decided to give it a try. She started small – each night before bed, she would sit for one minute and focus on her breathing.

After a week, Fran added another minute. Then she tried a short guided meditation on her phone. A few weeks later, she was meditating for 10 minutes each evening. What had begun as one mindful minute grew into a steady habit of calm.

Take your first step

What new habit would you like to have? What new habit would make a positive difference in your life? What's the smallest, simplest step you could start with today – one that feels doable? One that you can commit to consistently? Make it ridiculously easy. Whatever habit it is that you'd like to establish, begin with the easiest, most doable version. For example, rather than drink a glass of water before *every* meal, just drink a glass of water before *one* meal a day.

Commit to your small step for just one week:

This week, I will _____ every day.

Notice how you feel about it. Not whether you're doing enough, but whether it's something you can keep doing. When you start where success feels possible, you build confidence, consistency, and motivation which is the basis for lasting change.

A small win shows you that you *can* make changes; which makes further changes feel more achievable.

Perhaps you want to start writing a journal or you want to write a book. A novel or a memoir maybe? Aspiring authors often struggle with making writing a consistent habit.

So often, the hardest part of writing isn't the writing, it's getting started. Tell yourself you're just going to write for 10 minutes. That's all. Once you start, the chances are that you'll continue writing for longer. And if you don't continue? No problem. The important thing is that you've got started – you've started a new habit. Just empty your head of the words or ideas that come into your head. They don't have to be perfect. You can edit – re-write, change, add to it at any point.

By starting small, you don't have to rely on willpower and self-discipline, you can get started straight away.

Get started on that first step and, quite soon, the momentum takes over and you find yourself carrying on to the next step. All it takes is a little effort at the start. As Sir Isaac Newton discovered, objects at rest tend to stay at rest. But objects in motion tend to stay in motion. This is just as true for humans as it is for falling apples! When you take one small step, you create momentum and it's easier to continue. Take action and things will flow from there.

Small action – big change

An example from nature that illustrates how one small action makes a big difference comes from beaver dams. When beavers build a dam across a stream, it very slightly alters the water flow. But over time, that small change transforms the landscape, creating wetlands that support countless species.

The power of small steps

Small steps are effective for these reasons.

They require less self-control and willpower. Big changes require a lot of self-control, which is limited and easily drained. Small steps feel manageable and safe, rather than overwhelming, so you're much more likely to follow through.

They allow for easier adjustments. If something isn't working, rather than feel you've failed, you can easily adjust your approach based on what you've learned.

They build confidence. Each small success strengthens your belief that you *can* change. This boost in confidence makes it easier to take the next step.

They create consistency. Small actions are easier to fit into daily life and maintain consistently, which makes them more likely to stick.

They build momentum. Once a small change in behaviour feels normal, it's a firm foundation for the next step.

They make the process sustainable. Establishing a habit slowly but steadily helps develop and strengthen new neural pathways, which makes it much more likely that you'll stick with the new behaviour over the long term.

One step at a time

Many cultures tell stories that illustrate the fact that persistent, patient effort leads to positive results.

In Aesop's fable – *The Crow and the Pitcher* – a thirsty crow finds a pitcher with water at the bottom. It can't reach the water, but instead of giving up, it drops in pebbles one by one. Slowly, the water rises until the crow can drink. The story reminds us that together, small acts and persistence bring change.

And in another story – *The Dripping Drop* – often attributed to the philosophy of Lao Tzu and Taoist thought, a drop of water falls on stone, again and again. At first, the stone looks unchanged but over time, the water carves a hole right through the stone. Each single drop of water seems powerless, yet over time, it carves stone.

So too, your daily actions – small, repeated habits – can reshape your life.

'It'll take too long!'

If you're concerned about how long it will take before a habit becomes automatic, know that if you don't take action, time will pass anyway and nothing will have changed. Decide to start a new habit then ask yourself: 'How does taking this first step make me feel right now?' If it brings you a sense of hope or gives you focus, that's your signal to begin. Start with that first step and keep moving forward.

If, though, you don't feel optimistic or confident about taking that first step, you may need to make it even smaller. Try and work out what would be the smallest version – one that would move you in the right direction? That's all you need – a step in the right direction.

Get prepared

It could be that preparation is your first step. Preparing to start a new habit means setting the conditions for change before doing the new behaviour itself.

On pages 128–130 you will read that Professors DiClemente and Prochaska's Transtheoretical Model shows that behaviour change happens in six stages. Preparation is one of the stages.

A preparatory step could be to get support from others. You could tell someone you trust about your intentions or join a group or use an app that supports your new habit.

If you plan to get into the habit of eating more fruit and vegetables, a preparatory step would be to sharpen your chopping knife and buy storage containers for pre-cut vegetables. If you want to walk more, a preparatory step might be to buy some comfortable walking shoes.

Whatever it is, even though you haven't started the habit yet, preparation still counts as progress.

Key points

The limits of willpower

- The willpower needed to establish a good habit can be hard to sustain, as it requires effort, focus, and self-discipline – especially when you're stressed or tired.
- By starting small, you don't have to rely on willpower and self-discipline, you can get started straight away.

The power of small steps

- Small steps feel manageable, fit easily into daily life, and are more likely to be done consistently, helping to build momentum and make habits stick.
- All it takes is a little effort at the start. Take action and things will flow from there – you gain momentum and it's easier to continue doing it.
- Small steps allow for easier adjustments. If something isn't working, rather than feel you've failed, you can easily adjust your approach, based on what you've learned.
- Each small success strengthens your belief that you *can* change.

Preparation counts

- If you're still hesitating to take the first step, make it even smaller. Ask yourself what the smallest action is that would move you in the right direction. That's all you need – a step in the right direction.
- Preparation can be that first step: setting the conditions for change before starting the behaviour itself – and it still counts as real progress.

5
The Power of Habit Chains

The chains of habit are too weak to be felt until they are too strong to be broken.

—Samuel Johnson

In Chapter 1 you read that Professor Wendy Wood's research shows that habits aren't always driven by motivation, willpower, or rewards. Very often, habits are simply automatic responses that occur as the result of what she calls 'stable contexts'. That is, habits regularly occur at the same time, in the same place or situation, or in the same circumstances.

Professor Wood's study further reveals that nearly *half* of our daily actions happen in stable contexts. Together with her colleagues Jeffrey Quinn and Deborah Kashy, Professor Wood ran a study – published in 2002 in the *Journal of Personality and Social Psychology* – that involved asking participants to report their activities at random times throughout the day. Participants were alerted five times each day for one week using pagers (this was pre-smartphone days) and asked to write down what they were doing.

The data showed that about 43% of participants' actions were things they did regularly in the same context – the same place, time, or situation.

Participants' most frequently reported habitual behaviours included the following.

- **Eating and snacking** – for example, having breakfast or buying a coffee at the same time/place each day.
- **Commuting/travel** – taking the same route at the same time to college, work, or shops.
- **Household tasks** – cleaning, laundry, washing dishes, tidying.
- **Personal care** – brushing teeth, showering, grooming.
- **Media consumption** – watching TV at a set time or in a set place, reading the newspaper, checking messages.
- **Leisure routines** – exercising, walking, or unwinding in consistent times, ways, and locations.
- **Social connections** – for example, calling a family member at a particular time, chatting with the same people in the same contexts – the same time and place.

For most of us, then, nearly half of what we do each day happens out of habit. Our daily lives are built around routines that give structure and rhythm to our actions. This is important to know because it means creating a new positive habit becomes much easier when you link it to something you already do regularly.

There's a number of reasons why these natural anchors of daily life are relevant to starting a new habit.

- Built-in cues: when you link a new behaviour to something you already do – for example, practising balance by standing on one leg while brushing your teeth – you make it automatic. You don't have to rely so much on memory or willpower to make yourself do it.

- Less effort: it's easier to add a small new behaviour when you're already in the flow of something else, rather than making it a separate activity that needs a separate time, place, or level of energy.
- Habit chains: when habits are grouped naturally into your daily routines, they reinforce each other. Over time, with very little or no conscious effort, habit chains develop.

Habit chains

A habit chain is a phenomenon that forms when one action naturally leads to the next. Over time, these actions link together in a sequence – like the links of a chain – so that each step triggers the one that follows.

In Wood's 2002 diary study, researchers found that people's habits were often part of larger routines. For example, commuting consisted of a series of linked actions – leaving the house, locking the door, walking the same route, and catching the same bus – each one naturally following the last.

These chains are powerful because you only need to start the first link with a small action and the rest follow on from there. Over time, the whole chain runs automatically, each step cued by the one before it. Here's another example:

Arrive home → put the kettle on → make a cup of tea and have a snack → take the dog for a walk → return home and scroll through social media → make dinner.

Each step naturally leads to the next. There's a routine that runs on autopilot, guided by time, place, and the sequence of actions that came before it. This is very different from deliberate planning, where every action requires a conscious decision. For instance, a series of unrelated tasks like watering houseplants, then sending an email, making a cup of coffee, completing a job application, calling a family member, sewing a button back on a shirt, and then taking out the rubbish all demand separate conscious decisions, actions, and effort.

Habit chains reduce the need for decision-making because you don't have to think about what comes next. Each action cues the next, so once you start, the sequence flows with little effort.

You can use this to your advantage by linking a new habit to one you already do, making the new habit easier to start and maintain. The new habit is more likely to stick because it builds on the existing neural pathways of an already established behaviour.

This is exactly what Saskia, who you read about in Chapter 4, did. Saskia started with a 10-minute walk after lunch, three times a week. After a few weeks, her strolls turned into 20-minute brisk walks and she added another habit – listening to music or podcasts as she walked.

Saskia had started a habit chain. A month later, she felt inspired to do more. She started small, trying a short home workout twice a week. Over time, she gradually built up to regular walks and two to three strength sessions each week. The progression felt natural and sustainable, not forced. By increasing her activity slowly and steadily, she built a chain of habits in which each new behaviour strengthened the next.

Like Saskia, you can use the concept of habit chains as a deliberate strategy to build positive, supportive routines into your day. It's a simple method that helps new habits take root by linking them to actions you already do. When a new habit is attached to an existing one, the established habit is a cue, so you don't have to rely on memory, motivation, or will-power to make it happen.

For example, if you have young children, once you've dropped them off at school, you could attach a new habit – listening to a language lesson or podcast – on the walk or drive back home to work. And in another example, sending your last email and closing your laptop at the end of the day could become a cue do a short relaxation or breathing exercise and then go for a walk to help you to physically and mentally separate work from home life.

Keep a habit diary

By tracking your behaviours, you can discover how much of your daily life is made up of habits. A habit diary is a simple way to make yourself aware of the habits and routines that make up much of your day and, most importantly, highlights which habits and routines you could easily attach new habits to.

For one week, keep notes each day on these areas of your daily life.

- Eating and snacking.
- Commuting/travel.
- Household tasks.

- Personal care (showering, brushing teeth, etc.).
- Media consumption (TV, social media, podcasts, etc.).
- Leisure routines (hobbies, downtime).
- Social contact patterns (who you see or message and when).

Each time you do one of the activities, make a note of the time of day and what you did – for example, 'walked to work', 'checked Instagram', 'had a snack'. At the end of the week, look back and notice which things you do pretty much every day at the same time and in the same place.

By attaching a new habit – something you want to do – to something you already do, you help it become more automatic. Over time, this pairing makes the new behaviour easier to perform and means it requires little or no conscious effort.

Scheduling

A study by professors Veronika Brandstätter and Peter Gollwitzer ('Implementation Intentions and Effective Goal Pursuit' published in 1997 in the *Journal of Personality and Social Psychology*) shows that scheduling an activity makes it much more likely that it will get done. Brandstätter and Gollwitzer reported that 'difficult goal intentions were completed about three times more often when participants had furnished them with implementation intentions'.

In other words, you're much more likely to do something if you specifically identify when, where, and how you're going to do it. And the more specific you are about when, where, and how you'll do a habit, the more likely it is not only that you will do it, but that it'll stick.

If I . . . then I will . . .

When scheduling a new habit and linking it to an existing routine, you can use what Professor Gollwitzer termed the 'if–then' principle.

The 'if–then' principle (the implementation intention) involves deciding in advance exactly when you'll do something by linking a specific situation (the if) to a specific action (the then). Your brain doesn't have to think about whether or not to do something – it just recognises the cue and follows the intention automatically.

So, instead of saying, for example, 'I'm going to exercise more', you create a specific intention: '*If* I get the bus to work, *then* I will get off one stop earlier and walk'.

'If–then' plans a link to the situation: the 'If' – with a specific behaviour; the 'Then' – creating a strong mental link between cues and actions. So, when the cue is encountered, the behaviour is more likely to happen automatically. For example:

if I'm eating a meal, *then* I'll finish it with a piece of fruit;
if I'm having lunch, *then* I'll drink a glass of water;
if I get to the end of the week and I've received any payments, *then* I'll transfer 30% to my savings account.

Finding your best time for new habits – natural routines

New habits are even more likely to stick if you place them where they *naturally* fit into your day. This makes the habit feel like part of your routine instead of an add-on.

For example, if you want to eat more fruit, you don't need to choose a separate time in your day to do that. You could simply add a piece of fruit to one or more of your meals each day. Similarly, if you wanted to increase the number of steps you walk, rather than set a separate time each day to do that, you could lengthen your walk to and from work. And if you wanted to keep on top of recycling paper, plastic, and food packaging, rather than let it build up, each day when you leave the house, knowing that you walk past public recycling bins, you could take the previous day's paper, plastic, and packaging with you to dispose of.

Amira's meditation habit

After a few months of attending a morning yoga class, Amira noticed how calm and centred she felt afterward. She had recently become interested in meditation so she decided that she would spend just a few minutes meditating after yoga, while she felt relaxed and her mind clear. Linking the two things together felt natural – yoga flowed seamlessly into meditation. Within a few weeks, this simple addition became part of her routine, and the new habit became a natural part of her day.

Habits are like pieces of a jigsaw puzzle – new ones need to fit with the pieces already in place and slot naturally into your daily routine.

What new habit would you like to start doing? What context – what situation, time, or place – could make it flow naturally into your day?

Energy levels

It helps to be aware of your natural rhythms – the peaks and dips in your physical and mental energy and focus. By placing habits in alignment with your daily rhythms, your day naturally allows you to integrate new habits. However, life won't always give you the perfect conditions to build a new habit. Energy dips can make some habits – those that rely on physical or mental energy levels – feel harder to start and maintain. If the timing is wrong the habit is unlikely to stick, no matter how relevant the prompt.

You might, for example, feel most energised in the morning; but because of work, family, or other commitments you don't have the time and need to find other ways to consistently practice your new habit.

One solution is to do a shorter version. For example, if when your physical or mental energy is high, an hour of study or exercise isn't possible, you could maybe still fit in 10 minutes. Later in the day, when you have more time – even though your energy levels aren't so high – you can complete a longer session.

Another approach is to match the habit to your energy levels. If evenings are your only free time but your energy is lower, choose a lighter option – for example, doing yoga instead of strength training, or, if you're studying, reviewing notes instead of learning new material.

Tara and the morning study habit

Tara knew she was sharpest first thing in the morning, between 7 and 9 a.m. Ideally, she would spend that time period studying, but her new job required her to be online early. Instead of giving up her studies, Tara shifted her approach. Early each morning she spent 30 minutes researching and organising new material. Then, in the evening, when her energy was lower, she focused on light revision – summarising in writing what she'd learned. At the weekends, Tara spent the hours of 7–9 a.m. researching and writing her essays. It wasn't perfect, but it kept the momentum for her study habit alive and consistent.

Ali and the family-friendly fitness fix

Ali wanted to start running in the mornings, but with three young children, mornings were out of the question. Breakfast, packed lunches, school bags, squabbles, and missing shoes took up all the time before the school run. Instead of giving up, Ali decided that on the two afternoons after school when the kids were at football practice, he'd jog around the park until they finished. It wasn't the long morning run he'd have liked, but it fitted into his life. Over time, the short, consistent runs built his stamina and strengthened the habit.

The aim is to be consistent. When you arrange a new habit to fit your energy and routines, you have, once again, made it easier to do. And making a habit easy to do is what creates lasting change.

Key points

* Research shows that nearly half of what we do each day – eating and snacking, commuting, household tasks, etc. – happens out of habit. Our daily lives are built around routines that give structure and rhythm to our actions.

- This can mean that forming a new habit is easier if you link it to something you already do regularly.

Habit chains

- A habit chain is a phenomenon that forms when one action naturally leads to the next. You can use the concept of habit chains as a deliberate strategy to build positive, supportive routines into your day.
- Because you're building on an existing routine, the new habit takes less effort – you don't have to rely so much on memory or willpower to make yourself do it. It doesn't need a separate time, place, or burst of energy.
- The new habit is also more likely to stick because it builds on the existing neural pathways of an already established behaviour.

Habit diary

- A habit diary is a simple way to make yourself aware of the habits and routines that make up much of your day and, most importantly, highlight which habits and routines you could easily attach new habits to.

Scheduling: if–then

- Research shows that you're much more likely to do something if you specifically identify when, where, and how you're going to do it.
- By scheduling a new habit and linking it to an existing routine, you can use the 'if–then' principle. The 'if–then' principle involves deciding in advance exactly when you'll do something by linking a specific situation (the if) to a specific action (the then). Your brain doesn't have to think about whether or not to do something – it just recognises the cue and follows the intention automatically.

Natural routines and energy levels

- Habits are like pieces of a jigsaw puzzle – new ones are more likely to stick when they naturally fit into your day rather than feeling like an add-on.
- By placing habits in alignment with your daily rhythms, your day naturally allows you to integrate new habits. However, work, family, or other commitments may not always allow ideal conditions, so you'll need to find ways to practise your new habit consistently despite these constraints.
- Energy dips can make habits that require physical or mental effort harder to start and maintain. If the timing is wrong, the habit is unlikely to stick. To overcome this, shorten the habit (for example, try and fit in 10 minutes or so) or adjust it to match your energy levels by choosing a lighter version.
- The aim is to be consistent. When you arrange a new habit to fit your energy and routines, you have, once again, made it easier to do. And making a habit easy to do is what creates lasting change.

6
Make Your Environment Work for You

Successful people are simply those with successful habits.
—Brian Tracy

New habits need clear cues and triggers. Writing yourself a note creates an obvious reminder to act – such as putting out the bins on the right day, or locking the back door and unplugging devices at night. A Post-it note on the wall above your computer or kettle with a single word like 'breathe', 'meditate', 'stretch', or 'move!' can prompt you to do exactly that.

Another way to remind yourself to carry out a habit is to create visual prompts that remind you what to do.

When something is visible – like your toothbrush next to the bathroom sink or a phone charger on the kitchen counter – it becomes a cue that prompts you to do something – to brush your teeth or charge your phone. You don't have to remember do these things – because when you see your toothbrush, you brush your teeth; and when you see the phone charger, it reminds you to charge your phone. So putting what you need for a habit where you can easily see it greatly increases the chances that you'll follow through. A visible cue reminds you of your good intentions. The cue triggers the habit, even before you consciously decide to do it.

Donna's saxophone practice

Donna had always loved the sound of the saxophone but in recent years, as a result of work and family commitments, her saxophone lay untouched in its case. When she started working part time, she decided to start playing again. A friend gave her a simple piece of advice: 'Keep your sax somewhere you can see it. Let it remind you'.

So she did. She placed it on its stand in the living room. Any time she walked past or into the living room, it caught her attention. Now, she plays every day. Some days it's short bursts between clients or after the gym, other days it's a long two-hour session when she loses track of time.

What started as a visual cue – her saxophone in plain sight – has become an enjoyable part of her day.

What you see, you do

If, like Donna, you place what you need where you can see it, you're more likely to follow through simply because you've made what you intend to do – what you want to do – easier. You've deliberately created a prompt.

Here are some simple examples that can help you start and maintain good habits.

- A bowl of fruit on the kitchen counter or table reminds you to eat fruit.
- A water bottle on your desk reminds you to drink water.
- A book on the kitchen table, the sofa, or bed reminds you to read.

- Your running shoes near the door remind you to go for a run.
- Resistance bands next to your computer encourage a short spontaneous stretching or workout.
- A reusable shopping bag hanging by the front door reminds you to take your own bag.
- A compost container on the kitchen counter reminds you to compost food waste.

What is a habit you would like to start? What could be a visible cue that would help you to do the habit?

Set yourself up for success

Visual prompts remind you what to do. If you deliberately arrange and set up your surroundings, you can create associations that will cue habits and help you carry out your good intentions.

Whatever it is you want to do, spend a minute or two setting it up so that it's easier to go forward than not. Make the cue unavoidable. Want to go for a swim or a run each morning but can't get your act together? Then put your swimming costume or running gear out on a bedroom chair each evening and in the morning, put it on before you get properly dressed. That way you're far more likely to make a start. Try it, with no expectation other than to see what it's like.

Perhaps you want to eat more fruit, but are aware that you might not always get to the shops to restock the fruit bowl. Keep a couple of tins of fruit – apricots and peaches – and a bag of mixed berries in the freezer. That way, even when there is no fresh fruit in the house, you'll always have some fruit on hand to make it easy to maintain your new habit.

Kris's keys and lunch

Kris often started the week with good intentions. He'd prep a salad the night before, promising himself that tomorrow he'd eat well. But in the morning rush – coffee, bag, car keys, out the door – the lunch often stayed in the fridge. By midday, he'd be buying crisps and a sandwich from the shop.

So Kris made one small change: when he'd made his lunch he put his car keys in the fridge, next to his lunch. The next morning, he couldn't leave the house without his keys or without taking his lunch too. His trick worked – he ate a healthy lunch, saved money, and felt pleased with himself for being so smart!

Audio prompts

When your environment and surroundings provide a clear visual or physical cue, you don't have to remember to do something. The cue does the prompting for you. But it's not only visual prompts that help you build habits – sound prompts can be useful too. A gentle alarm can remind you to do habits that need to happen at a specific time but that in the flow of the day are easy to forget, like drinking a glass of water, taking a short breathing break, or standing up to move if you sit for long periods. You can set a soft reminder on your phone and, once the habit is established, you might find you don't need the alarm anymore.

Habit settings

Do you have a specific chair or place on the sofa where you read, eat, or watch TV? Perhaps the car is where you listen to music or a podcast – you don't go to the car specifically to listen to podcasts and music, but when you *do* get in the car you habitually play music or a podcast.

As Wendy Wood's research shows, habits are strongly shaped by context: the time and place you're in often influence what you do. This means that you can deliberately organise places and spaces in your home so they are linked to specific habits, making those behaviours more automatic. For example, you might create a calm corner with an armchair, cushions, a throw, and soft lighting. Sitting there could prompt reading, meditation, or focused breathing. Or you could set up a table in one corner of a room that is used only for studying or focused work. Even something simple – like sitting in the same chair every morning with your coffee – can link that place to a few minutes of quiet reflection.

Commit – and make backing out harder

Setting up visible and audible prompts and setting up spaces and places for specific habits can help make a habit easier to start. But you can also set things up so that there are consequences if you don't follow through.

Making a commitment helps ensure you act on your intentions, or at least makes it harder to back out. It bridges the gap between intention and action by introducing clear consequences or incentives that encourage follow-through. Here's few ways that you could try.

- Schedule the habit with someone else (a walk, workout, or study session).
- Join a group or class with fixed times.
- Tell a friend or partner or group chat what you plan to do and when. Agree to pay them £20 if you don't follow through.
- Donate to a cause you like if you miss the habit.
- Pay in advance for classes, sessions, or courses.
- Give yourself a reward which you only get after you've followed through on your commitment (more on this in Chapter 7).

Making a pledge – an agreement with yourself – works because it adds structure, accountability, and consequences. This makes it easier to act on your intentions and harder to ignore them.

Key points

Visual and audio prompts

- Visual prompts remind you what to do. If you put what you need for a habit to happen where you can easily see it, it increases the chances that you'll follow through. A visible cue can trigger the habit, even before you consciously decide to do it.
- Sound prompts can be useful too. A gentle alarm can remind you to do habits that need to happen at a specific time but, in the flow of the day, are easy to forget.

Habit settings

- Research shows that habits are strongly shaped by context: the time and place you're in often influence what you do. This means that if you deliberately organise places and spaces in your home around specific habits, you can make it more likely that those habits will become automatic.
- If you deliberately arrange and set up your surroundings, you can create associations that will cue habits and help you carry out your good intentions. You don't have to remember to do something. The cue does the prompting for you.

Commit – and make backing out harder

- You can also set things up so that *not* doing the good habit takes more effort than doing it, by adding consequences if you don't follow-through. This makes it easier to act on your intentions and harder to ignore them.

7
Enjoyment and Rewards

The hard must become habit. The habit must become easy. The easy must become beautiful.

—Doug Henning

Many of us have habits we want to start – things we feel we *should* do but don't feel motivated to actually do. Maybe, for example, rather than face a messy kitchen each morning you want to get into the habit of clearing up straight after dinner. Or you want to make it a habit to get off the bus two stops early and walk the last part of the journey. But you just can't seem to get it together and do it.

So what to do? The key is to make the habit both enjoyable and rewarding enough to do so that you want to do it. You can do this by pairing the task – something you *should* do – with something you *want* to do – something enjoyable.

Research shows that this makes it far more likely that you will do it. In 2011, University of Pennsylvania's Professor Katy Milkman and her colleagues carried out a study ('Holding the Hunger Games Hostage at the Gym' published in the *Journal of Management Science* in 2014) the results of which showed that using a strategy called 'temptation bundling' – pairing a less appealing behaviour with a desired activity – significantly increases follow-through rates. Over a period of 10 weeks, they tested three conditions.

Full temptation pairing: Participants got access to audiobooks only when at the gym.

Intermediate condition: Participants had access to the same audiobooks but could use them outside the gym too. They were, however, encouraged to restrict their listening to the times when they were in the gym.

Control group: Participants received a gift card for an audiobook but no pairing up instructions.

The results showed that those in the group that paired visits to the gym with an audiobook visited the gym 51% more often than the control group. The intermediate group had a 29% increase in attendance compared to the control.

Although, over time, attendance fell after the study ended, 61% of participants were, none the less, willing to pay to restrict their audiobook access so it was only usable at the gym. They recognised that limiting access to a pleasurable activity – the audiobook – helped them stick to a good habit – exercising.

The study highlights the fact that motivation isn't something you wait for – it's something you can create. When a habit like exercising or decluttering and tidying is something you want to start but you're reluctant to do, the key is to link it with immediate satisfaction so that you see it as something worth doing *now*, not just something you'll benefit from at some point in the future.

The habit of clearing up straight after dinner, for example, could be paired with the task of listening to a podcast or music while you're clearing up. In fact, you could keep the enjoyable activity as something you do only when you need to do the unappealing task – listen to podcasts *only* if you get off the bus and walk the rest of the journey. And in another example, watch a show you enjoy *only* while walking or running on the treadmill.

Create small, instant rewards

You can further increase the chances of sticking with a new behaviour if you give yourself an immediate reward right after you do it.

Rather than relying on future rewards and benefits – telling yourself, for example, 'if I keep going to the gym I'll be fitter in six months' – a small, instant reward makes the behaviour feel satisfying now. And that encourages you to repeat it.

If, for example, you made a New Year's resolution to go for run each day before work, the hard part might not be the running, it could be leaving your warm bed. But you could make a deal with yourself: 'After I've been for a run I'll buy a coffee and pastry to take home with me'.

We all have things that give us pleasure and moments of happiness. Which of these activities could act as a small incentive and reward for you?

- Watching a short, funny video or episode.
- Spending time on a hobby or interest.
- Reading a few pages of a book or magazine.
- Playing a word game, a video game, or scrolling through social media.

- Sitting in the garden on a sunny day.
- Drinking a favourite coffee.
- Having a favourite snack.
- Enjoying a bubble bath or a hot shower.
- Chatting on the phone with a friend or family member.
- Adding another tick on a habit tracker.

Whatever it is that you enjoy doing, rewarding yourself with small pleasures keeps your brain engaged in a habit loop – cue, habit, reward – which is key to maintaining a habit.

What is a habit you want to start? Before you begin, decide what enjoyable activity you'll pair it with and a small immediate reward you'll give yourself after you've completed the habit.

Robin's kitchen cleaning habit

After putting her children to bed and finishing other chores, Robin struggled to clean and tidy up kitchen at the end of the evening. But she wanted to come down to a clean kitchen in the morning. So she found a way to make the task enjoyable while doing it. She created a number of 'cleaning playlists' – songs that she enjoyed listening and singing along to.

Then she added a reward afterwards – 15 minutes on the sofa with a hot chocolate before she went to bed. Soon the music made starting easier, the reward made finishing satisfying. Robin had established a positive routine and cleaning the kitchen stopped feeling like a battle. What used to be a chore became a habit that fitted naturally into her evening.

Anticipating a reward

In Katy Milkman's study, follow-up interviews suggested that it wasn't *just* the enjoyment of listening to the audiobook during the workout that motivated participants in the study, it was also the anticipation of finding out what happened next in the story they were listening to. Looking forward to hearing the next chapter made participants look forward to going to the gym. The pleasure of anticipation turned gym sessions from something they *had* to do into something they *wanted* to do – something to look forward to.

When you make your new habit something you actually look forward to, you're far more likely to stick with it. In fact, the anticipation and desire themselves can be just as powerful – sometimes even *more* motivating – than the reward itself. Thinking about or seeing cues related to a rewarding activity can trigger a dopamine release. Your brain learns that the cue is a signal that something good is coming and that surge of dopamine motivates you to take action to get the reward.

Research by Stanford University's Professor Brian Knutson and his colleagues (published in 2001 in the *Journal of Neuroscience*) showed that key dopamine centres light up most strongly when anticipating a reward (like money or food), rather than when receiving it. Dopamine doesn't just make you feel pleasure; it motivates you to seek it. That's why the good feelings that come with, for example, looking forward to a meal out with friends can feel as pleasurable as the time with the friends and the meal itself.

Another example of anticipation driving a good habit is when you are looking forward to going to bed so that you can continue the book you're enjoying reading. Or consider online shopping: receiving a message telling you that your order will arrive that day gives you a small dopamine burst. The pleasure is in the anticipation, not just receiving the item.

Make anticipation work for you: turn anticipation into motivation

The fact that dopamine is released when you imagine and look forward to something enjoyable means that you can make the process work for you. You can train your brain to feel motivated before you carry out the habit.

For example, if you wanted to motivate yourself to go for a walk each evening after dinner, you might plan to make it enjoyable by listening to music or chatting to a friend on the phone while you walk. You might also plan to reward yourself with a small treat afterwards.

The anticipation must, though, be followed through with an action!

Because your brain gives you a small dopamine hit just for imagining listening to a podcast or chatting on the phone to a friend during the walk and the reward afterwards, you'll feel good before you've even started, so there's a risk that you could lose the will to act because your brain thinks you've already done it.

Quite simply, anticipation works best when it leads to action.

Alain's running habit

Alain wanted to get back into the habit of running again. One weekend he thought about how he could best motivate himself to start the habit – he'd pair his runs with a true-crime podcast and reward himself with a healthy cooked breakfast. Just imagining himself jogging through the park, listening to a gripping story, and eating breakfast afterward made him feel good before he'd even started.

But he went to bed late that night and the next morning, the imagined motivation had gone. There was no real structure in place: Alain hadn't set out his running clothes, chosen a time, planned a route, or made himself accountable by telling anyone he was starting. When his alarm went off, getting out of bed and running was definitely not what he wanted to do.

The positive feelings from planning had made him feel good and made his brain think he'd already made progress. Without anything in place to pull him into action, he hit snooze, then snoozed again, and told himself he'd start tomorrow. But without any strategies to help support his intentions, nothing happened.

Alain's plan would, though, have succeeded if rather than just thinking about it, he'd created the conditions that make action easier than inaction. Here's what would have made it more likely that he would turn intention into action.

- Preparation: Plan a simple route, put out running clothes, and have the podcast ready to play.
- A small first step: Just get out of bed. Then get dressed. The next step is to run for just five or ten minutes.

- Make himself accountable: Run with a friend. Or tell a friend his aim and promise to pay them £10 if he doesn't follow through.

The right support makes the habit feel inevitable. Although Alain felt inspired and motivated when he imagined the run and the reward afterwards, running depended entirely on how he felt when he woke up. Without any preparation, his morning mood decided everything. But once he built in simple supports and set things up the night before, the path was clear – he just had to step onto it.

Alain's experience makes it obvious that habit success is consciously created, not just felt. Rather than rely on fleeting motivation, you can also make the same shift by adding structure, clear cues, and small reliable wins.

Build enjoyment and rewards into your own habit

What is a habit that you want to start or strengthen?

My habit: _____

What could you add to make it enjoyable while you do it?

While I'm doing it, I'll enjoy: _____

What small reward could you look forward to having right after completing your habit?

I'll reward myself by: _____

What supports will you put in to make sure the new habit happens? Attach it to a current habit or routine.

I will support the new habit by: _____

Variable rewards

When you receive the same reward every time you complete a habit, dopamine levels rise, but they do eventually level off. However, when the reward – the timing, size, or type of reward – is uncertain, your anticipation is heightened and dopamine surges are stronger.

The concept of variable rewards is known in behavioural psychology as the 'intermittent reinforcement' principle. With intermittent reinforcement, the behaviour is still strengthened by rewards, but not each and every time. Far from demotivating you, the uncertainty becomes motivating. The unpredictability keeps you engaged and coming back, motivated by the possibility that *this* time, you might get the reward.

Gambling is the most obvious example of variable rewards. Slot machines, scratch cards, and betting systems are all designed around intermittent reinforcement. Each bet, each play, each pull of the lever brings the possibility of a win. And if it doesn't, players repeat the behaviour with the hope that next time *will* be a win. The unpredictable rewards keep them hooked.

Variable rewards more commonly show up in other areas of our lives. For example, the following.

- Social media: Random notifications, likes, friend requests, messages, and comments are a deliberate design tactic that encourages constant checking and continuing interaction in the hope of a 'reward'.
- Retail stores and cafes: Loyalty programmes often use variable rewards – surprise money off coupons, discounts, and offers – to ensure customers are engaged and keep coming back. The middle aisles in Lidl and Aldi supermarkets, for example, are stocked with limited-time offers ('When it's gone it's gone') that change weekly. These non-food 'special buys' – tools, garden gadgets, clothing, kitchenware, toys, or random seasonal items – encourage customers to browse just in case there's something new or surprising. The unpredictability makes people curious – they never know what they'll find there.
- Games and apps: Random bonuses, rewards, and 'loot drops' keep you motivated and engaged.

How Instagram and Duolingo build habits

Instagram
Variable rewards can keep people alert and engaged with a service or product. Here's how Instagram – the social media app for sharing photos and short videos – keeps people engaged by combining cues, simple routines, and variable rewards.

- Cue: Push notifications to alert users to a new post, 'likes', and messages.
- Routine: Users engage in the routine of scrolling through their feed and interacting with content by

---

liking, commenting, sharing, and posting photos and videos. An endless stream of content with no natural stopping point – scrolling easily turns into long sessions.

- Reward: The habit is further reinforced by unpredictable rewards, such as likes and comments or a great post. You never know what you'll get, so constant checking keeps you engaged.

Together, these features stimulate the brain's reward circuit, creating feelings of pleasure and motivation and reinforcing a habit loop – driven by notifications, endless content, and unpredictable social feedback – that millions of people repeat several times a day.

Duolingo

Duolingo is a language-learning app also used by millions of people around the world. It doesn't just teach languages – it builds habits of daily practice by applying well-established principles of habit formation. Duolingo creates a habit loop for its users in the following ways.

Cues and prompts

- Goals – the app prompts learners to set a goal when you start, so there's a built-in trigger to practice every day.
- Push notifications – short, clickable pop-up messages – are sent by the app to a user's device with reminders like 'Don't break your streak!' which act as external cues.
- Visible prompt – learners can keep Duolingo on their home screen, making it a visible prompt.

Routine

- Small steps – lessons are designed to be short and accessible, allowing users to learn in small, manageable steps.

(Continued)

Rewards

- Digital rewards such as points, gems, and badges.
- Streak counter: Daily learning creates a run. However, if you miss a day and don't complete your lesson, you normally lose your streak (your count of consecutive days practised). Since streaks are one of the strongest habit motivators in the app, to keep users engaged, Duolingo offers 'Streak Freeze' – an item you can buy with in-app currency (gems). If you've bought a Streak Freeze in advance and then miss a day, your streak is 'protected', and you don't lose it.

Create your own variable rewards

Predictable rewards can eventually lose their appeal, but varied unexpected rewards keep a habit alive. You can use this to your advantage by creating your own system of small, variable rewards that make the habit feel fresh and that you will genuinely enjoy.

Write a mix of small rewards on individual slips of paper: a favourite tea or coffee, a snack you love, an episode of a show, a podcast, a chat on the phone with a friend, a short walk, or any other small pleasure that appeals to you. As well as small enjoyable treats, you could add a couple of bigger treats – such as a supermarket curry or a takeaway for that night's meal.

Put the slips into a jar or use a randomiser app. Each time you complete your habit, draw one at random. The surprise element keeps the habit rewarding – and keeps you coming back.

Another way to keep a habit fresh and enjoyable is to add variety to the habit itself – exploring different running and walking routes, different workout playlists, a new podcast series, new recipes for healthy eating. The habit stays the same, but the small pleasures and rewards change, keeping it interesting and giving your brain something to look forward to each time.

Tiered rewards

One more idea that helps with keeping you motivated is to use tiered rewards. With tiered rewards you reward yourself according to how much time – how many days or weeks – you've kept up the habit.

A medium streak of one week could be rewarded with, for example, a favourite meal, watching a film, buying a new magazine or book, a new app or game. A longer streak of one month or more could be rewarded with a bigger reward – a meal out, something new to wear, a workshop, class, or experience you've been wanting to do.

Tiered rewards support habit formation because they provide meaningful incentives and rewards and create a sense of progress. Habits are easier to maintain when you can see improvement over time.

Tiered systems make progress visible and motivating: the more consistently you perform the behaviour, the more you benefit. This sense of momentum encourages you to keep going and reinforces the habit as it develops.

Key points

Making a habit enjoyable and rewarding

- Pairing a new habit you feel you should do with something you enjoy makes it far more likely that you'll do it. You're more likely to see the habit as something worth doing.
- As well as pairing a new habit together with something you enjoy doing, you can further increase your motivation if you give yourself a reward right after you complete it.

Anticipating a reward

- When a new habit is something you look forward to, you're far more likely to follow through, as anticipation can be just as motivating as the reward itself.
- However, because your brain gives you a small dopamine hit just for imagining and anticipating the enjoyment and reward, you'll feel good before you've even started, so there's a risk that you could lose the will to actually do the habit because your brain thinks you've already had the enjoyment and reward.
- The anticipation must be followed through with an action! You're more likely to follow through when anticipation of the enjoyment or reward is supported by conditions that make action easier than inaction, such as clear cues, small steps, and a supportive context.

Variable rewards

- Predictable rewards can eventually lose their appeal but varied unexpected rewards keep you engaged and coming back. You can use this to your advantage by creating your own small, variable rewards that make the habit feel fresh and something that you'll genuinely enjoy.

- Something else you can do is add variety to the habit itself. The habit stays the same, but how you do it and the enjoyable things you pair it with change, keeping it interesting and something to look forward to each time.

Tiered rewards

- With tiered rewards you reward yourself according to how much time – how many days or weeks – you've kept up the habit.
- Habits are easier to maintain when you can see improvement over time. Tiered rewards make progress visible and motivating: the more consistently you perform the behaviour, the more you benefit. This sense of momentum encourages you to keep going and reinforces the habit as it develops.

8
Identity, Habits, and the People Who Influence Them

We first make our habits, and then our habits make us.
—John Dryden

Lasting habits aren't just driven by rewards; they also depend on how well the behaviour reflects who you are or want to become.

Habits that match how you see yourself are known as 'identity-based habits'. In contrast, habits that focus on a specific end goal are known as 'outcome-based habits'.

Identity-based habits are more effective than outcome-based habits because they change how you see yourself, not just what you're trying to achieve. With an identity-based habit, if, for example, you see yourself as 'someone who hikes', you naturally act in ways that confirm it. This could involve owning walking boots, appropriate clothes, and equipment for hiking, regularly going out walking and hiking even when it's cold and raining. You might also belong to a walking group. You see yourself as a walker or someone who hikes. If, though, you were walking with a specific goal in mind, maybe to train for a sponsored walk, once the goal was achieved – you completed the sponsored walk – you might stop going for regular walks. It was an outcome habit.

You don't see yourself as a hiker, the walking was simply to train for a sponsored walk.

Outcome-based habits often lose momentum after the goal is reached. In contrast, identity-based habits are for the long run. They are a natural part of your daily life.

Six ways that identity-based habits are more effective than outcome-based behaviour

Habits and a positive self-identity are mutually reinforcing. The more you perform a habit that aligns with how you see yourself and who you are becoming, the more you gain evidence that this identity is true – that this *is* what you do and who you are. If you consistently go to the gym, you provide evidence for the identity of being a 'healthy person'. This motivates and encourages you to continue the habit, creating a positive feedback loop that further reinforces the identity. Who you are is what you do. And what you do is who you are.

Identity habits are automatic. Outcome habits are goal orientated. They often need self-discipline and willpower to make them happen. On the other hand, identity-based habits are automatic. They're not separate behaviours you have to think about and make yourself do. If you see yourself as a healthy eater, you automatically eat healthy snacks. If you see yourself as an organised person, you might have a habit of tidying your desk at the end of each working day. You don't think about whether or not to do it – you do it because it's who you are.

Identity habits are internally motivated. Because identity habits are simply what you do and who you are – unlike goal-orientated habits – they are not so dependent on external motivators and rewards. For example, someone who's aiming to lose 10 kg in the next few months might have a strict meal plan and weigh themselves every day. Any time the weight loss fluctuates – as it naturally does – it's easy to feel despondent: 'It's taking too long. I'm not getting anywhere. It's too hard'. In this example, motivation depends entirely on an external factor – the number on the scales. Progress fails because the habit isn't part of the person's identity – it has a singular specific goal.

In contrast, someone who sees themselves as a healthy, active person and would like to lose some weight is likely to simply up their game to match who they already are. After work they might walk a longer route home and go for a cycle ride at the weekends, cut down on carbohydrates and sweet snacks. They act in line with their identity; by focusing on how they see themselves instead of the weighing scales, they are likely to lose the weight. The habit sticks because it's part of their lifestyle.

Identity habits can better manage challenges. You are more likely to persist with a challenging habit when the habit relates to your sense of who you are. Someone who identifies as 'a runner' will continue running even when the weather is bad or inconvenient in some way; while someone who's just 'trying to run more' will find reasons to avoid a run.

Identity habits manage setbacks. With outcome-based habits, the process can feel like a test of self-control, willpower, and discipline. Missing a couple of steps can feel like failure. 'I missed two classes so I might as well stop going'. With identity-based habits, if you miss a day or two, you see it as an exception – it doesn't put you off your stride – you simply pick up from where you left off. It's easier to restart because it's what you do and who you are. 'I missed two classes but I'm going back tomorrow'. Your self-image as, for example, 'someone who exercises' or 'someone who is learning Italian' stays intact.

Identity habits influence other habits. If, for example, you start seeing yourself as a health-conscious person, you naturally make healthy food choices, prioritise physical activity and exercise, ensure you have enough rest and sleep, and generally take better care of yourself, without having to focus on each habit separately.

Beth's before and after story

Before: 'I'm just not an organised person'.

Beth was convinced that being organised simply wasn't who she was. Other people seemed to plan easily and keep everything under control, but she always felt behind. Her mornings started in chaos as she reacted to whatever suddenly felt urgent. Tasks took longer than she expected, and she spent the whole day trying to catch up. By the end of the day, she felt drained and guilty about whatever she hadn't got done. Every day seemed to confirm the same belief: *I'm just not someone who can stay on top of things.*

After: 'I'm becoming an organised person'.

Beth's shift in identity began with a small commitment: a five-minute review at the end of each day. She wrote down

---

what did and didn't get done and what would now need doing the next day – what would be a priority, what was important or urgent and what could wait. That simple routine gave her a sense of direction and control that she'd not had before. She left work calmer and arrived the next morning with purpose instead of panic.

After a week, Beth realised she wasn't lurching from one task to another anymore. She felt steadier, more focused, and more in charge of her time. She began to see herself as someone who was becoming organised. By the end of the month, even her colleagues commented on how much calmer she seemed. Gradually, Beth's old self-image faded. She wasn't the person who struggled to stay on top of things anymore, she was someone who was organised, capable, and in control.

Who do you want to become?

> We are what we repeatedly do.
>
> —Aristotle

Choosing the person you want to become is a powerful way to build new habits. Reflecting on – and writing down – your responses to the following four questions can help guide the process.

Decide on an outcome goal
Write down what you want to achieve. For example:

'I want to be more organized'. 'I want to be stronger'. 'I want to be more mindful'. Your outcome goal _____

Turn your outcome goal into who you want to become

For example, someone who wants to be stronger: 'I want to become someone who does strength training'. Someone who wants to be more mindful and present more: 'I want to become someone who is mindful and present'.

Your identity: I want to become someone who _____

Choose one small step that helps reflect this identity

For example: a small step for someone who wants to become a fitter, stronger person could be to do five chair squats each day. Someone who is becoming more mindful might meditate for two minutes each morning or commit to eating one meal per day without digital distractions.

Your action: One small thing I can do today that aligns with my new identity is: _____

The key is to start small. Each small action is a step forward for the person you want to be. As you consistently take these actions, you build evidence for yourself that this is who you are becoming. Over time, that evidence strengthens both the identity and the habit that supports it. This makes it easier to continue the habit because it now feels like a natural part of who you are.

Create an affirmation

The first time you perform your new habit, write down an 'I am becoming . . .' statement. For example: '*I am becoming more mindful and present*' or '*I am becoming stronger*'.

These are not affirmations about who you already are – they're statements about the direction you're growing in. Saying 'I am mindful and present' might not feel true yet. But saying 'I am becoming mindful and present' *is* true, because it reflects the positive approach you are taking.

Your affirmation: I am becoming _____

Put a note with your affirmation somewhere prominent – where you can see it each time you carry out your new habit.

Habit tracking

Habits are easier to maintain when you can *see* improvement – you can see that you are becoming the person you want to be. A paper-based daily habit tracker – a diary or calendar – is the simplest approach. Simply add a tick for each day you complete the habit. And don't berate yourself if you miss a day or two. (More on this in Chapter 9.)

Habit tracker apps also make progress visible and create identity-based motivation. The more you do the behaviour, the more you see your progress and the more evidence you have that you are the person you want to be. Popular habit tracking apps are 'Productive', 'Streaks' (for iPhone users), and 'Habitica' (turns building habits into a game).

How other people shape your habits and who you become

Identity isn't only shaped by your own actions, your family and friends play a role too. Your social environment influences your behaviour – it sets the standard for what's normal, what feels rewarding, who you think you are and how you fit in.

You pick up habits simply by being around other people. If your family, friends, or colleagues are active, eat healthy meals, or regularly make time for hobbies, those behaviours feel normal and sustainable. And if you get together with others who share the same interests – whether it's walkers, writers, artists, or any other group – you become part of a community that shares similar habits. The sense of belonging makes the habit feel natural.

Role models

Identity-based habits and role models are closely connected. The person you want to become is often shaped by the people you admire – they can influence who you want to be and the habits you want to adopt.

Who do you admire? What good habits do they practise? Role models give you a living example of who you want to be: 'I want to be someone who meditates like they do', or 'I want to be a reader like them'.

When you see someone consistently living a habit you admire – going to the gym for example, or reading every day, or simply doing daily word puzzles – it shows you what's possible and points you in the direction of the kind of person you could be. The identity comes first, and the habits follow.

Learn the habit from someone who does it

By observing someone's routines and asking about their process, you get a good idea of what it takes to practise that habit yourself.

Think of someone you know who does a habit you'd like to adopt. It could be related to health, fitness, studying, reading, creativity, or anything else.

Talk to them about it. Ask:

- How and why did you start?
- Where does this habit fit into your day or week?
- What would you recommend as the easiest first step?
- What helps you keep going when you don't feel like it?

Learning about their specific strategies and how they manage any difficulties gives you guidance and ideas that you can use to start doing the habit yourself.

Harley's role model

Having recently recovered from a broken ankle, Harley decided she wanted to get stronger and improve her balance, but although she'd tried, she felt out of place at a gym. One day, she saw her neighbour Elena – who was in her 60s – carrying heavy shopping like it weighed nothing. 'You're stronger than I am!' said Marley 'What gym do you go to?' Elena smiled and said 'Oh, I don't go to the gym. I just live my life. Carrying shopping, gardening, housework – it all keeps me fit'.

Harley was inspired. She decided to make a start. Once a week, rather than have her supermarket order delivered, she collected it herself. She picked up the bags one in each hand and walked slowly to her flat keeping her posture steady – just like she'd seen Elena do.

(Continued)

Soon, she started adding small strength-related habits to her day. She walked up the escalator at the tube station and took the stairs at work. At home, she stood on one leg while brushing her teeth. When she reached for something from a low cupboard she did a deliberate squat each time. If she was waiting for the kettle to boil, Harley did slow heel raises at the counter; and while waiting for her dinner to cook, she leaned against the worktop and did 10 gentle push-ups. Nothing took too much time or effort, she was simply living more actively.

A few weeks later, as she carried two bags of shopping up the stairs without stopping, Elena spotted her. 'See? Strong already', she said.

Support from other people

Support from other people can make a big difference in maintaining good habits, both practically and psychologically.

When others ask about your progress, and encourage you or share similar goals, their interest and positive feedback helps make a new habit feel rewarding while emotional support helps you bounce back from setbacks and get back on track.

If you tell a friend you've started taking part in the five km Park Run every Saturday, their interest confirms your identity as a runner. You're aware that others see you as someone who is active and who runs. Their interest also creates accountability. When people see you as someone who keeps fit and healthy, you're more likely to act accordingly.

Surround yourself with people who make you happy. People who make you laugh, who help you when you're in need. People who genuinely care. They are the ones worth keeping in your life. Everyone else is just passing through.

—Karl Marx

Find your tribe

Habits can be easier to maintain when shared with others. Seek out other people who support your goals by joining groups that already meet regularly, like book clubs, sports teams, exercise classes, or creative groups. Or you could start your own group and invite others to join you. You could also join an online community that shares your interests and follow creators and influencers who model the habits you aspire to. Podcasts, YouTube channels, and newsletters can also provide examples, guidance, and motivation to keep you on track. When the people around you reflect the same identity as you, the habits that reinforce that identity become much easier to maintain.

Key points

Identity-based habits vs outcome-based habits

- Identity-based habits are more effective than outcome-based habits because they don't just focus on what you want to achieve, they change how you see yourself.
- Outcome-based habits often need self-discipline and will-power to make them happen. They are often dependent on external motivators and rewards. Because they focus

on short-term goals, they tend to fade or stop after the goal is achieved.

- In contrast, identity-based habits are automatic. They're not separate behaviours you have to think about and make yourself do. They're long term – they're a natural part of your daily life. They influence and support other similar related habits – one good habit often encourages other related habits.
- Because identity-based habits are tied to who you are, setbacks are easier to handle – missing a day or two is not a big deal; it's easy to pick up the habit again because it's who you are and what you do.

Mutually reinforcing

- The more you perform a habit that aligns with how you see yourself and who you are becoming, the more you gain evidence that this identity is true – that this *is* what you do and this *is* who you are.
- This motivates and encourages you to continue the habit, creating a positive feedback loop that further reinforces the identity.

Small steps, affirmations, and habit tracking

- The key is to start small. Each small action is a step in the direction of the person you want to become.
- Repeating an 'I am becoming . . .' affirmation each time you do the new habit helps reinforce your new identity, strengthens your self-belief, confidence, and motivation.
- Using a habit tracker – a diary, calendar, or a habit tracker app – makes progress visible. The more you do the behaviour, the more you see your progress and the more evidence you have that you are the person you want to be.

Social support

- Identity isn't only shaped by your own actions, your family and friends play a role too.
- Your social environment influences your behaviour – it sets the standard for what's normal, what feels rewarding, who you think you are, and how you fit in.
- Other people's interest, support, and encouragement make new habits feel rewarding and create accountability. Their support can also help you recover from setbacks and get back on track.
- Role models provide a living example of who you want to be. By observing their routines and asking about their process, you get a good idea of what it takes to practise that habit yourself. You can ask them about specific strategies and how they manage any difficulties.
- When the people around you reflect the same identity as you, the habits that reinforce that identity become much easier to maintain.
- Seek out people who practice similar habits, whether in groups, communities, or online platforms like podcasts, YouTube channels, newsletters, or through influencers and creators, to gain examples, guidance, motivation, and a sense of belonging.

9
Reflect and Adjust

You change best by feeling good – not feeling bad.
—BJ Fogg

To determine if a new habit is working, it's helpful to reflect on your progress – to consider what's working and what's not, what difficulties you may have encountered, and what might need adjusting.

Here's some questions to ask yourself.

- Have I been doing the new habit as regularly as I intended – daily or weekly? If yes, what helped?

  It might, for example, have been a clear cue or because you attached the habit to an established routine. Or maybe it was because it started with a small step or ended with a small reward.

- Are the results, even if small, evident? In what way?

  Notice small wins. If the habit is reading, perhaps you finished two chapters by the end of the week. If the habit is mindfulness or breathing exercises, maybe you've noticed yourself feeling calmer during stressful moments. If the habit is practising a skill, you might be making fewer mistakes than when you started. Even tiny changes count – they're proof the habit is working.

- Is the habit becoming easier and more automatic or do I need to tweak it to make it easier?

  If something isn't working, it's not *you* that failed, it's the process. Don't let a relapse make you give up! Instead, try and identify why it happened. What can you learn from that? What will you do differently from now on? Rather than think 'I can't do it', ask 'how can I make it easier?' You might, for example, need to make it smaller. Instead of a 30-minute walk, shrink it to a 10-minute walk. Instead of eating five pieces of fruit each day, eat three. Or just one. Remember, small versions keep the identity intact: 'I'm someone who does this habit'.

The six stages of change

Be patient and be kind to yourself. Don't berate yourself if you have a setback. Meaningful change takes time – and accepting that allows you to build a habit at a steady, realistic pace. When you're willing to invest that time, you create a strong foundation for even more positive habits to grow.

Research from the 1980s by Professors DiClemente and Prochaska shows that behaviour change happens in six stages. Although originally focused on quitting smoking, their Transtheoretical Model explains that the same psychological process applies to any habit you want to stop or start – whether you're trying to quit smoking, be more physically active, eat more healthily, or build any new routine.

DiClemente and Prochaska identified that change is not a single event but a process, moving through six stages.

- **Pre-awareness** – not thinking about change.
- **Contemplation** – thinking about change.
- **Preparation** – getting ready to act.
- **Action** – starting the new habit or behaviour.
- **Maintenance** – sustaining it over time.
- **Progress, change, and relapse** – restarting the process.

Pre-awareness. In this first stage, you're not even aware that you need to or can make any changes. If you don't think a problem exists, you won't be motivated to make any changes. You might, for example, think 'I know health and fitness are important but it's not something I care about'.

Contemplation. At this stage you are thinking about starting a new habit but are not committed to action. You probably weigh the pros and cons – the benefits and effort required. You want things to be different, but may not be sure if you can make a change or how to go about it.

Preparation. This stage may involve several different steps such as:
- looking for signs and evidence that you should make changes;
- looking for ideas and information about how to behave differently;
- understanding what you need to do;
- knowing what you're aiming for.

In the preparation stage, you intend to make some changes but you may feel that certain things – a simple plan, environmental supports cues, rewards, etc. – need to be in place before you can make changes.

(Continued)

If you understand what you need to do and you can foresee the benefits, if you feel that making a change aligns with your needs, abilities, and identity – who you want to be – you are more likely to get started.

Action. This is the stage where you get started – actively practising the new habit. Small wins, an element of enjoyment, immediate rewards, and support are all important.

Maintenance. By this stage, you've established the new way of behaving. You're now focused on maintaining the habit, and it's becoming more stable and automatic. You've internalised the change: and can see yourself as 'I'm someone who . . .'.

Progress, change, and relapse. A successful change in thinking or behaviour usually involves moving from one of these stages to the next. Each stage is preparation for the next one, so hurrying through or skipping a stage may not be as effective as progressing from one stage to the next. However, DiClemente and Prochaska's Transtheoretical Model acknowledges that you might slip up and revert back to your old way of thinking and behaving.

If you do relapse it's unlikely that you will completely fall back to where you began. You may well take two steps forward and one step backward, making progress and losing ground, learning from mistakes and using what you have learnt to move forward. It's entirely possible that you will go through the cycle more than once before the new way of thinking and behaving becomes established.

Know that things develop in their own time. Habits often require several attempts and adjustments before sticking. Don't think of difficulties as failure; instead, think of setbacks as part of the process of change: opportunities to learn, do better next time, and build your confidence.

There's a reason habits are often referred to as something you 'practise'. You get the chance to do it over and over – to create little shifts and changes that evolve into helpful habits. Understanding that setbacks are normal and to be expected will help prevent difficulties from undermining your determination and confidence.

David's six steps to better sleep habits

Pre-contemplation. Over the last few months, David struggled to wake up each morning and then spent the rest of the day feeling tired. But he blamed it on recent pressures at work. When his partner suggested that, actually, he needed a better wind down routine and an earlier bedtime, he dismissed it.

Contemplation. After several more weeks of dragging himself through the day, forgetting things, snapping at colleagues, and struggling to focus, David realised he couldn't go on like this. He wasn't quite ready to do anything about it, but he *was* starting to recognise it was a problem and that something had to change.

Preparation. David decided to take a small step and see how it went. No screens for the last 20 minutes before bed and, instead, he would read a book – something light and easy by a favourite author. And he'd turn the light out by 10.30 p.m.

Action. The first week went well – David left his phone in the kitchen and spent 20 minutes reading in bed before he turned the light out by 10.30 and went to sleep. He felt pleased with himself. Gradually, his evenings settled into a calmer rhythm.

Maintenance. Within a few weeks, David had a steady wind-down routine: around 9 p.m. he drank tea instead of

(Continued)

another glass of wine. Before going to bed, he put his phone in the kitchen, then had a shower to relax him. He then read for 20 minutes and turned the light out by 10.30 p.m. He felt less tired, more alert, calmer, and more present at work.

Progress, change, and relapse. Some months later, due to concerns about a health problem, David slipped back into old habits and found himself doom scrolling in bed instead of reading. His sleep unravelled, and the familiar fatigue returned. But he recognised what was happening and a week later, he was back to his established routine and within days he felt more settled again.

David's approach worked because he took it one small step at a time. He built confidence with small wins. When his routine slipped, once he was aware of the lapse, he simply went back to the beginning.

Start again with a beginner's mind

Beginner's mind is a concept from mindfulness. It tells us that when it comes to difficulties and challenges, whatever did or didn't happen, whatever went wrong before is in the past. And the past has gone.

Beginner's mind encourages you to let go of beliefs and judgements about what did or didn't happen and instead, approach each moment anew. You put the past behind you and step into the present. In fact, you are only ever in the present.

A missed day or a missed week becomes just that: a missed day or a missed week, not proof that the habit is broken.

You can see a slip up as coming from the 'old you' and use a fresh start to motivate the 'new you' to move forward.

Whatever mistakes you made, however many days you missed, that was then. This is now. Instead of thinking 'I've failed' or 'I always mess this up', beginner's mind prompts you to ask yourself 'What have I learnt from the past that can help me begin again today?'

Use the word 'but'

If you slip up and miss a day or two – even a week or two – rather than tell yourself 'I've missed the habit too many times now', don't stop there. Instead, add the word 'but'. The word 'but' naturally shifts your thinking toward a positive next step: 'I didn't . . . *but* I can . . .'. For example: 'I didn't practise playing my guitar the last few evenings . . . *but* I can pick it up again this evening'. And in another example: 'I haven't been to the gym for a couple of weeks . . . *but* I can start again tomorrow'. Adding the word 'but' helps you acknowledge the setback without being stuck in it. While shifting your focus toward to what positive step you can take next.

The million-dollar question

The question everyone asks is: *How long does it actually take for a habit to become automatic?* Unfortunately, there's no single, reliable answer. That's because habit formation depends on several factors that vary from person to person and even from habit to habit. Here's why.

Not all habits require the same effort. Some habits, such as adding a glass of water or a piece of fruit to lunch, are simple and quick to repeat. Others, such as exercising three times a week, require planning, time, or emotional effort.

Everyone's starting points differ. People begin new habits from different starting points. A lot depends on how familiar or comfortable the behaviour already feels. For example, if you're someone who cycles regularly and you decide to start running too, the habit could be easy to take up. But if you aren't physically active to begin with, turning running into a consistent habit can be more challenging.

A supportive environment is crucial. A supportive environment – clear cues, an easy set up, few distractions – encourages steady progress. But an unsupportive environment creates difficulties and slows things down. Habits don't form in a vacuum – they form inside your everyday life. Changes in family and work commitments, stress, or illness can also create difficulties.

Rewards matter. Habits form faster when the reward is immediate and meaningful.

Identity plays a role. When a habit fits your identity – when it feels like 'this is who I'm becoming' – it becomes automatic more easily. Habits that don't feel like who you are take longer and require more support.

Steady, even progress is key. A new habit will become automatic not because a certain number of days pass, but because you repeat it consistently in an environment that supports it. Even if you slip up and miss a few days, what matters is that you return to the habit and continue doing it. The key is consistency, not waiting for a number of days to have passed.

Habits that don't become automatic

Some habits quickly become automatic and start to feel like part of who you are. Others, however, never seem to get there, no matter how long you practise them.

This often happens when a habit doesn't align with your environment, your routines, or your natural way of behaving. In these cases, the habit may always require conscious effort or come with some discomfort. And that's okay. It isn't a failure on your part; it simply means the habit will likely need ongoing reminders, support, or structure to be maintained.

Over the last 15 years, whenever I'm writing a book my routine is to write every single day. Sometimes it's for 30 minutes, sometimes it's for several hours. Writing every day is a habit. And usually, for me, it's an effort. But I have support in place.

I start small – I tell myself I'll just write for 20 minutes or so and then have a short break. I sit and write where the light is brightest – in the kitchen in the morning and in the bedroom in the afternoon. I can't concentrate for long periods, so I have constant breaks and small rewards – a cup of tea and a chocolate biscuit, for example, or a short walk or a chat on the phone with a friend.

If my environment or daily routine changes – as it has when I've been staying at my friends Chris and Sue's place to cat-sit – I adjust my schedule to fit the new setting so I can keep my daily writing habit going.

If, like me, you need supportive strategies and behaviours to keep a habit alive, it doesn't mean you're failing – it means you're being realistic. You understand and accept that these supports act like scaffolding, helping to keep the habit steady and more likely to happen, even if it never becomes fully automatic.

If, for example, you still see yourself as someone who doesn't like exercise, that identity will eventually pull you back to old habits. Which is why you need supportive strategies to help you maintain the habit.

Key points

Reflect

- Reflecting on your progress helps you to see what is and isn't working and what might need adjusting.
- Meaningful change takes time – and accepting that allows you to build a habit at a steady, realistic pace. When you're willing to invest that time, you create a strong foundation for even more positive habits to grow.

The six stages of change

- Research shows that behaviour change is a process, moving through six stages. Each stage is preparation for the next one.
- Even when you've established a new habit, there's a chance you might slip up and revert back to your old way of thinking and behaving. It's unlikely, though, that you'll completely fall back to where you began.

- It's possible that you will go through the cycle of behaviour change more than once before a new habit becomes established. And that's okay.

Beginners' mind

- The mindfulness concept of beginners mind tells us that whatever went wrong before, it's in the past. And the past has gone. Whatever mistakes you made, however many days you missed, that was then. This is now.
- See a slip up as coming from the 'old you' and use a fresh start to encourage the 'new you' to step back up again.

Use the word 'but . . .'

- If you miss several days or weeks, rather than telling yourself, 'I'm hopeless, I didn't do (the habit)', add the word 'but'. This simple shift helps you acknowledge the setback while focusing on the positive next step: 'I didn't . . . *but* I can . . .'.

The million-dollar question

- How long a habit takes to become automatic varies from person to person and from habit to habit. This is because habits differ in the effort they require, and everyone begins from a different starting point.
- How supportive your environment is, how enjoyable and rewarding the habit is, your personal situation – responsibilities and commitments – and how well the habit aligns with your identity also determines how quickly a new habit becomes established.
- A new habit will become automatic not because a certain number of days pass, but because you repeat it consistently in an environment that supports it.

Habits that don't become automatic

- Some habits quickly become automatic and start to feel like part of who you are. Others, however, never seem to get there and may always require conscious effort or come with some discomfort.
- It simply means you will need ongoing reminders, cues and rewards, supports and structures in place to help you maintain the habit.

PART THREE

Why Bad Habits Persist – and How to Change Them

10
Breaking Bad Habits

To change a habit, make a conscious decision, then act out the new behaviour.

—Maxwell Maltz

Jamal told himself that vaping was just something he did – a few puffs as he walked to and from work, at lunchtimes, and then in the evening before dinner. At first, it didn't seem like a problem. But the habit grew without him noticing. His vape was always in his pocket, always in his hand, always within reach. He'd catch himself having a puff without remembering he'd picked it up.

Jamal shared a house with three others and one evening, after stepping outside more than once to vape, he realised that once again, he'd missed half the conversation with his housemates. Jamal realised his habit wasn't small anymore. Not only was it anti-social, it was bad for his health. Things needed to change but he didn't know where to start.

Like Jamal, you might have a habit you want to change. Perhaps you have a habit of snacking on unhealthy foods or a habit of impulse buying online. Maybe you spend the evenings sitting on the sofa, watching TV, scrolling through your phone, and staying up too late. Perhaps you regularly drink alcohol, use recreational drugs, or smoke and you'd like to stop.

Many of us have one or two habits we'd like to break. For example, a 2025 UK government report – 'Applying All Our Health' – states that over half (52.7%) of smokers in England want to quit. So if we know something's bad for us, why can't we just stop?

Once a habit is formed, it becomes resistant to change, especially when the same cues, contexts, routines, rewards, and identity – your sense of 'who I am' – remain in place. This is good news for positive habits and bad news for negative ones.

The key to change is understanding the system that created the habit and intentionally rewiring it. That means developing strategies to counteract the existing patterns. Change requires conscious effort: interrupting automatic responses by disrupting old cues, routines, and rewards and creating new automatic pathways. It isn't easy – but it is possible.

Understanding why bad habits form and persist

Understanding why bad habits form and persist helps explain why they can be so hard to break.

Habits aren't inherently 'good' or 'bad' – they're simply behaviours your brain repeats because they serve a purpose. They might help you stay safe or healthy, reduce stress, save energy, alleviate boredom, or create a feeling of comfort or pleasure. Whatever the habit, your brain learns that the behaviour leads to a specific outcome, so it repeats it automatically.

However, there is one crucial difference between good and bad habits: compared to good habits, bad habits are much better and faster at providing rewards.

> Good habits have immediate costs and delayed rewards; bad habits have immediate rewards and delayed costs.
> —James Clear

Before we look at how to break a bad habit, here's a reminder of how habits form. In this chapter, the focus will be on how theories about habit formation relate to bad habits.

The habit loop

Charles Duhigg's habit loop explains how habits form through a repeating cycle of cue, routine, reward. A cue – such as the time of day, an emotional state, a location, or an event – prompts a routine; for example, reaching for a snack during a TV ad break or biting your nails when you feel anxious. The reward is the positive feeling that follows the behaviour, such as pleasure, distraction, or a sense of relief.

This automatic connection between the cue and the reward strengthens the habit loop. Every time you repeat a habit, your brain strengthens the neural pathway associated with it and your brain defaults to that behaviour – even if it's unhelpful or harmful to you in some way.

The role of dopamine

Dopamine is the brain chemical linked to motivation, pleasure, and reward. Pleasurable behaviours release dopamine, which reinforces your desire to repeat them. As you repeat a behaviour – even if it's an unhealthy habit, such as doom scrolling or overeating – your brain recognises it as rewarding or relieving.

The anticipation can be as powerful – or even more motivating – than the reward itself. Just thinking about or encountering cues related to a habit can trigger a dopamine release, making the habit more likely to persist.

In time, wanting the reward ('I *need* it') can become stronger than the actual liking ('I enjoy it') of the reward. For example, craving a cigarette or vape even though it no longer feels satisfying.

This wanting is a craving – a strong urge that pushes you to seek something out. The intense wanting is one of the key reasons addictive behaviours – like drug use, gambling, or other compulsive habits – continue even after the pleasure they once provided has faded. You can read more about addictions on pages 185–187.

Variable rewards

When a reward is consistent – when you always get the same reward – dopamine levels increase but, eventually, they level off. However, when the reward is uncertain in some way – timing, type, or size – your brain releases more dopamine than it would for predictable rewards. The anticipation and uncertainty keep you engaged in the behaviour because you're hoping that this time, you'll get the pay off.

Intermittent rewards are a double-edged sword. Used positively, they can boost motivation, learning, and growth. But they can also fuel bad habits and addictive behaviours.

Gambling, endlessly scrolling through social media, constantly checking your phone for notifications, or staying glued to a game for hours are all a result of intermittent rewards; you stay engaged in the hope of receiving the rewards – positive comments, likes, random bonuses, loot drops, and wins. Each unpredictable reward keeps the dopamine system active and reinforces the habit loop. This unpredictability is what makes some habits so addictive and hard to stop.

Context – time, place, and circumstances

Not all habits are driven by rewards. Our surroundings and environment can reinforce habits – both good and bad. Often, the context – such as the time, place, or situation – serves as a powerful cue that triggers the habit.

Once a habit is formed, we often repeat it without thinking about why we're doing it or what the outcome is. The habit becomes automatic, requiring little or no motivation or conscious sense of reward – it's just something you always do in certain situations without thinking about it. If, for example, you eat chocolate every time you watch TV in the evening, the habit isn't just driven by an enjoyable reward. It's triggered by sitting on the sofa (the place) in the evening (the time). The environment itself prompts the behaviour. Your brain learns the cues – when and where the habit happens – and will repeat it automatically, even when the original reward is no longer obvious.

Habit chains

If a habit has become part of a routine, it gets embedded in a habit chain – a sequence of actions where one action or behaviour is automatically followed by the next.

For example, you might finish dinner, then move to the sofa with another glass of wine, switch on the TV, start playing a video game, get some snacks, return to the game, and end up staying up later than you intended. You only need to start the first link in the chain and the rest follows automatically.

Emotional and psychological needs

Bad habits often begin when certain cues or emotions become linked to behaviours that feel good or relieve discomfort. When our emotional needs aren't being met, we often fall back on unhealthy habits to fill the gap, which is why the cycle keeps repeating.

Comfort eating, for example, can temporarily soothe feelings of stress, sadness, or disconnection – but it doesn't address the underlying issues. As a result, the cycle keeps repeating.

Over time, dopamine-driven reward pathways reinforce these behaviours, while emotional coping and rationalisation keep them going. Even when you know a habit is harmful, it's easy to justify it to avoid feeling guilty – telling yourself 'I've had a difficult day, I deserve this' – and this kind of reasoning makes the habit feel acceptable and allows it to continue.

Mental effort

The process of establishing good habits often requires effort now for benefits later – making them harder to maintain without self-discipline or specific supports being in place.

Saving part of your income, for example, requires self-control in the present and could mean giving up short-term treats like a coffee on the way to work, meals out, or trips away. The reward – being able to afford something bigger or more meaningful or future financial security – comes much later.

In contrast, bad habits are easily formed and maintained because they're convenient, satisfying, and offer immediate rewards. Instead of saving, you might be tempted to buy things on impulse because it feels good at the time. This immediate pleasure makes the habit easy to repeat, even though it might cause stress or financial problems later.

In a number of studies over recent years, Florida State University's Dr Roy Baumeister and his colleagues have discovered that making decisions and choices, taking initiatives, and suppressing impulses all seem to draw on the same well of mental energy.

Your brain only has so much headspace. When that capacity is taken up by daily tasks, demands, and responsibilities, there's less energy left for making helpful decisions or resisting temptations. Of course, you do have a measure of self-control, but it's not unlimited. When you're stressed, overwhelmed, upset, hungry, or tired, your brain's ability to resist temptation weakens. In those circumstances, it naturally falls back on automatic behaviours because they require less effort. These default habits are the easy, well-worn path your brain takes when it's already overloaded and willpower and self-control are low.

You might, for example, be trying to break the habit of drinking wine while watching TV and watching 'just one more' episode in the evening. But after a day full of decisions – work pressures, family responsibilities, and constant demands – your brain is overloaded. Your ability to think clearly and exercise self-control is drained.

When you're mentally exhausted, your brain takes the easiest route: it defaults to the familiar routine of a couple of glasses of wine and binge watching – even though you know that long term it isn't what's best for you.

Mel's evening scrolling habit

One Sunday evening, Mel told herself that starting tomorrow she wouldn't immediately start looking at her phone after dinner. She wanted to break that habit; to spend her evenings cooking a nice meal, then relaxing – without returning to endless scrolling – reading, watching a film or, in the summer, doing some gardening.

The first couple of days went well, but on Wednesday when she arrived back home, her brain was overloaded. The day had been filled with meetings, details, and deadlines. So after a quick meal, when her phone buzzed, her tired brain didn't argue and Mel just reached for it.

She didn't consciously decide to flop onto the sofa and start scrolling her phone after dinner – it just happened. Her mental energy had run out. Her brain simply followed a well-worn path of least resistance.

She felt drained and annoyed with herself. 'I'm not even choosing this, I'm just too tired to do things differently'. The problem wasn't her willpower – she was too tired to do things differently.

Identity shapes your habits

Bad habits become even stronger when your self-image supports them. If, for example, you tell yourself or other people, 'I always smoke when I'm stressed', you're more likely to do just that. It becomes a self-fulfilling belief, and you behave in line with it.

Do you ever think or say any of the following about yourself?

- I'm a smoker. I've been smoking for years.
- I'm not an active person.
- I don't like exercise. It's just not me.
- I'm someone who eats or drinks when I'm stressed.
- I'm the kind of person who always runs late. That's just who I am – I can't change it.
- I can't keep things tidy – it's just not me.
- I'm the kind of person who can't just have one (drink, cigarette, cake, etc.).
- I'm terrible with money. It's just the way I am.

- I'm always on my phone, that's just me.
- It's a habit. I can't help it.

These common self-identity statements reinforce unhelp-ful habits.

The phrases make the behaviour strengthen your belief that 'this is who I am', which makes it harder to change. The process works in reverse, too. Your beliefs about yourself are a result of behaviours that you've repeated over time. Each time you overspend or make an impulsive purchase, for example, or have a drink or smoke because you're stressed, you reinforce those self-beliefs.

You are what you think. And what you think, you are.

Key points

Good habits and bad habits

- Once a habit is formed, it becomes resistant to change, especially when the same cues, contexts, routines, rewards, and identity – your sense of 'who I am' – remain in place. This is good news for positive habits and bad news for negative ones.
- Habits aren't inherently 'good' or 'bad' – they're simply behaviours your brain repeats because they serve a purpose.
- However, there is one crucial difference between good and bad habits: compared to good habits, bad habits are much better and faster at providing rewards.

- Understanding why bad habits form and persist helps explain why they can be so hard to break. The following is a reminder of the theories of habit formation and how they relate to bad habits.

The habit loop

- Habits form through a simple three-part cycle: cue → routine → reward.
- Over repeated cycles, the habit loop becomes faster and more automatic because the neural pathway is well established.
- Pleasurable behaviours release dopamine, which reinforces your desire to repeat them. As you repeat a behaviour – even if it's an unhealthy habit – your brain recognises it as rewarding or relieving.
- In time, wanting the reward ('I *need* it') can become stronger than the actual liking ('I enjoy it') of the reward.
- This wanting is a craving – a strong urge that pushes you to seek something out. The intense wanting is one of the key reasons addictive behaviours continue even after the pleasure they once provided has faded.

Variable rewards

- When a reward is uncertain in some way – timing, type, or size – your brain releases more dopamine than it would for predictable rewards. The anticipation and uncertainty keep you engaged in the behaviour because you're hoping that this time, you'll get the pay off.
- Used positively, variable rewards can boost motivation, learning, and growth. But they can also fuel bad habits and addictive behaviours, such as gambling.

Context – time, place, and circumstances

- Not all habits are motivated solely by rewards. For many habits, context – time, place, and circumstances – plays a key role.
- Once established, a habit becomes automatic and no longer needs conscious motivation or reward. Repeating a behaviour in the same context strengthens the mental association, making the habit – whether it's a good or bad habit – increasingly automatic.

Habit chains

- If a habit has become part of a routine, it gets embedded in a habit chain – a sequence of actions where one action or behaviour is automatically followed by the next. You only need to start the first link in the chain and the rest follows automatically.

Emotional and psychological needs

- When our emotional needs aren't being met, we often fall back on unhealthy habits to fill the gap, which is why the cycle keeps repeating.
- Even when you know a habit is harmful, it's easy to justify it to avoid feeling guilty – telling yourself: 'I've had a difficult day, I deserve this'. This kind of reasoning makes the habit feel acceptable and allows it to continue.

Mental effort

- When you're stressed, overwhelmed, hungry, upset, or tired, your brain looks for the easiest option and defaults to automatic behaviours. In these states, even though you know they're not good for you, bad habits are hard to resist because your brain has less energy for self-control.

Identity shapes your habits

- Bad habits become even stronger when your self-image supports them. If, for example, you tell yourself or other people: 'I'm not an active person, I don't like exercise. It's just not me' it becomes a self-fulfilling belief, and you behave in line with it.
- The process works in reverse, too. Your beliefs about yourself are a result of behaviours that you've repeated over time.

11
How to Break Bad Habits

A change in bad habits leads to a change in life.

—Jenny Craig

Self-awareness

Understanding how bad habits are formed and established is the first step to breaking them. The next step is to identify the cues, triggers, and context, the routine, rewards, and identity associated with a habit you want to break.

You could track the habit for a week – write down when, where, and why the habit happens. At the end of the week, ask yourself the following questions. Your answers can help turn what might feel like a daunting challenge into something you can better understand, plan for, and change.

Cues and triggers

- What's the cue – what prompts the habit?
- Where and when do I do the habit?
- What am I usually doing right before the habit starts?
- What, if anything, do I usually feel beforehand? Stress? Tiredness? Boredom? Loneliness? Something else? (This question helps you think if the habit is serving as an

emotional coping strategy. If it is, you can then be aware of high-risk moments instead of being caught off guard.)

The reward

- How do I feel immediately after doing the habit?
- What do I gain, what benefit do I get from this habit? Enjoyment? Comfort? Distraction? Relief? Social connection? (Certain habits are tied to bonding – for example, smoking or vaping breaks, drinking with friends, shared complaining.)

Understanding the specific reward a habit provides can help you to replace it with something healthier that meets the same need.

Identity

What do I tell myself about the habit? What reasons or justifications do I tell myself and other people?

Set intentions before setting boundaries

A common mistake people make when trying to change or break a habit is jumping straight to restrictions – cutting back on screen time, for example, by deleting apps, setting timers, or scheduling phone-free hours – without first getting clear on *why* they want to make the change.

So, do ask yourself questions.

- Why do I want to stop doing this habit?
- What do I want less of? (Stress, guilt, time wasting, tiredness, frustration?)

- What do I want instead? What do I want more of? (This shifts your focus from losing something, to gaining something – benefits such as time, money, improved health.)
- What kind of person do I want to be?

Answering these questions helps you clarify why the change matters to you, what the habit is currently costing you, what you have to gain, and how it connects to the person you want to become.

Instead of, for example, telling yourself 'I need to stop checking my phone so much', ask yourself *why* you want to stop. Maybe you've realised that constant checking breaks your attention, making it hard to focus on work or study or engage with other people or whatever else is going on around you. Perhaps you want to stop the habit because you don't like how it makes you feel – checking news, messages, and social comparison makes you anxious. It could be that you don't like what the habit takes away from your life – it feels like your phone is controlling your attention instead of the other way around. The phone is choosing what you think about next. What you want instead is a sense of space, calm, and agency over your thoughts. You want to be someone who is present and engaged with who and what is around you.

Thinking about what you want less of, what you'll gain, and who you want to become helps you see that your intended habit change is going to be an act of self-care, not one of discipline and punishment.

Positive thinking

Behaviour change is far more effective when you define your aims in positive terms rather than negative ones. If your aim is to 'stop eating junk food', your mind focuses on the word 'stop'. But intentions built around 'can't', 'mustn't', or 'stop' don't serve to inspire you. A more effective approach is to focus on what you *do* want, rather than what you don't want. Instead of saying, 'I must stop eating junk food', reframe it around a positive identity: 'I want to eat healthier food'. This shifts the focus from restriction and emphasises a supportive, healthy action.

When you think about changing a habit in terms of what you want rather than what you don't want, you create a more sustainable approach. It feels optimistic and empowering, not restrictive or punishing, and your mind becomes more willing to accept and move toward the change.

Small steps

Trying to quit a habit in one go can feel overwhelming – it can seem too big and too hard to manage. In contrast, taking small, gradual steps makes the process more manageable, which makes it more likely that you'll start and keep going.

If, for example, you wanted to stop drinking so much coffee, a first small step could be to replace your second or third coffee with a herbal tea or another hot drink you enjoy. And if you want to stop scrolling on your phone late at night, your first step could be to put your phone in another room and leave it there, 20 or 30 minutes before you go to bed. And in another example, if you feel you're drinking too much alcohol in the evenings, a simple first step is to get yourself a glass of water before pouring your usual drink, and sip that first.

In Chapter 4, you learned why taking small steps is an effective way to build a good habit. The same principles apply when breaking a bad habit. Here they are again.

Small steps are effective because of the following.

They require less self-control and willpower. Big changes require a lot of self-control, which is limited and easily drained. Small steps feel manageable and safe, rather than overwhelming, so you're much more likely to follow through.

They allow for easier adjustments. If something isn't working, rather than feel you've failed, you can easily adjust your approach, based on what you've learned.

They build confidence. Each small success strengthens your belief that you *can* change. This boost in confidence makes it easier to take the next step.

They create consistency. Small actions are easier to fit into daily life and maintain consistently, which makes them more likely to stick.

They build momentum. Once a small change in behaviour feels normal, it's a firm foundation for the next step.

They make the process sustainable. Changing a habit slowly but steadily helps build and strengthen new neural pathways, which makes it much more likely that you'll stick with the new behaviour over the long term.

Concerned about how long it will take to break a habit? Know that if you don't take action, time will pass anyway and nothing will have changed. Decide to make a positive change in your behaviour and then ask yourself, 'How does taking this first step make me feel right now?' If it brings you a sense of hope or gives you focus, that's your signal to begin. Start with that first step and keep moving forward.

If, though, you don't feel optimistic or confident about taking that first step, you may need to make it even smaller. Try and work out what would be the smallest version – one that would move you in the right direction. That's all you need – a step in the right direction.

Get prepared

It could be that preparation is your first step. Preparing to stop a habit means setting the conditions for change before trying to change the behaviour itself.

On pages 128–130 you will have read that Professors DiClemente and Prochaska's Transtheoretical Model shows that behaviour change happens in six stages. Preparation is one of the stages.

Answering the questions on pages 159–161 about breaking a bad habit – the cues, contexts, and rewards, why you want to change, what you want more and less of, and who you want to become – is a good first preparatory step.

Another preparatory step could be to get support from others. You could tell someone you trust what you're trying to change, or join a group, or use an app that supports habit change.

Even though you haven't begun to break the habit yet, this preparation still counts as progress.

Change your environment

A survey carried out in 2023 by furniture store DFS discovered that 78% of respondents tended to eat their evening meal on the sofa, with 19% stating that this is how they always eat their dinner. Alongside this, while 84% of parents agreed that family meals were important, only 50% of family dinners were eaten together. And even when these dinners are being eaten with everyone physically present, at least 66% said that they will be on their mobile phone rather than talking with those around them.

Maybe you're someone who eats dinner on the sofa and you'd like to change that habit. What you'd like instead is for you and your partner or family to sit at the table, eat together, and catch up on each other's day. However, the kitchen table has become a dumping ground, covered in junk mail, magazines, your laptop, keys, charging cables, and children's toys. It's just easier to go and sit on the sofa.

By deliberately organising the spaces in your home, you can make supportive habits easier. In this example, you could start by clearing the table, then add one or two items that encourage the habit of eating your meals at the table – such as a fruit bowl, candles, a table runner, or placemats. Doing this also acts as a preparatory step – you haven't started the new habit yet, but you have taken a first step.

The aim is to make bad habits harder to do and good habits easier. One effective way to do this is to link specific habits to specific places, which makes them easier to remember and perform consistently. For example, if you're often stressed looking for your keys before leaving home, place a small tray or bowl to put your keys in on a hallway table or shelf or install hooks by the door. Having a designated spot encourages you to put your keys away as soon as you come in, so they're always easy to find when you leave.

When a place becomes associated with a habit, the environment does the reminding for you. That reduces reliance on willpower and helps good habits stick while making unwanted habits less automatic.

Mel's habit change

Environmental cues influence your behaviour – for better or worse – and their effect becomes even stronger when your brain is too tired or overloaded to make different choices. Let's go back to Mel who in Chapter 10 wanted to change her habit of collapsing on the sofa after dinner and scrolling though her phone for most of the evening – but was often too tired to do anything else.

Mel decided to make things easier for herself – she changed her environment.

She did this by creating a small corner in her living room: an armchair, a soft throw blanket, a small table, and a book by one of her favourite authors. She put her phone charger in the hallway ready to plug her phone in and leave it there.

Monday after work, she was tired as usual, but she was also looking forward to her new routine. Everything she needed for a calm evening was already waiting for her – visible and easy to access. After dinner, she made herself a mug of tea, sat in the armchair, and opened her book. And she relaxed.

Make it harder to do

Remember, the aim is to make bad habits harder to do. Another way to do this is to make cues and triggers less visible.

Out of sight really can mean out of mind. When you make a cue less visible or less convenient, you make it far less likely that you'll be prompted to repeat the habit. So, to weaken a habit loop, remove the associated cues and triggers. Here are some ideas.

Excessive screen use: Delete distracting apps from your phone. Turn off notifications for apps. Unplug the TV or keep the TV remote control in another room. Put your phone into Sleep mode after 10 p.m. Put your phone, laptop, or remote in a drawer or in another room. At night, keep a charged phone in your bedroom[1] but place it out of reach – on the floor or on a separate table or chest of drawers – rather than beside your bed. Use an analogue alarm clock instead of your phone to avoid the temptation of scrolling before going to sleep or as soon as you wake up. The idea is that doing any of these actions adds extra steps so using screens becomes less automatic.

Create a motivational screensaver: an image of what you could be doing with the time that you're spending on your phone. It could be a photo of your family, friends or pet, a hobby or interest, landscape or garden. It could simply be a motivational quote.

---

[1] *UK fire and rescue services suggest keeping a charged phone in your bedroom for emergencies. However, they advise against charging phones or other devices overnight because lithium-ion batteries and chargers carry a small but real fire risk. They recommend charging devices only when you are awake and present.*

Snacks and sweets, soft drinks: Don't buy them! But if they are in the house, put them in the back of a cupboard so they're not so visible. And, if you always stop for a coffee and a pastry on your way to work and you want to break the habit, take a different route so that not only do you not see the coffee shop, you avoid it entirely.

Impulse spending using credit cards or online shopping apps: Remove saved payment details or uninstall shopping apps. This can help slow down impulsive online shopping.

Top tip

Want to avoid late night snacking? Then brush your teeth earlier in the evening.

What objects or cues in your environment make a bad habit easy for you to do? What could you move out of sight? What could you do so that the habit becomes inconvenient?

Replace the habit

> A nail is driven out by another nail; habit is overcome by habit.
> —Erasmus

Your brain forms habits by linking a cue – such as an emotional state or a time or place – to a behaviour – the habit – and then to a reward. But when you stop a habit, you create an empty space in that loop. If the cue is still present, your brain still expects something to happen. But unless you replace the habit with a new behaviour, you're then relying on self-control to avoid slipping back into the old habit.

Perhaps your job involves frequent short periods of downtime – waiting for customers or clients – and during those moments you automatically reach for your phone. You might decide that in those quiet periods you will stop the habit and simply *not* look at your phone. But without something else to fill that empty space, the cue (boredom) and the reward (distraction) are still there, pulling you back to the phone scrolling habit.

Mina's change of habit

Mina is a barber. Whenever she had a five- or ten-minute gap before her next client, she automatically pulled out her phone and began scrolling through social media. It was simply what she did whenever there was nothing happening.

One day, Mina decided she wanted to break the habit. But instead of trying to stop scrolling altogether, she gave herself something better to do. She'd recently booked a holiday to Italy for later in the year, so she chose to use those short waiting periods to learn Italian.

Now, whenever she feels the urge to pick up her phone, she opens her language app instead.

A replacement behaviour fills that gap in the loop – the cue and reward remain, but the habit has changed to a more positive behaviour.

You might, for example, decide you want to stop binge watching TV series – that you want to watch one episode a night instead of three or four. If you have a replacement habit ready, you'll need less self-control and willpower because you have an alternative behaviour to turn to. In this example, you need a clear stopping point, so after one episode, you could turn off the TV, get up off the sofa, and start a wind down routine – make a hot drink, have a shower, brush your teeth, and get into bed with a book to read. Binge-watching often happens because you just *have* to know what happens next. A fun idea would be to turn off the TV and before going to bed, writing down what you think will happen in the next episode.

A replacement habit creates new neural pathways which eventually give your brain a new automatic action to take when the old cue appears.

You'll need to get prepared: decide in advance what you'll do – what your replacement habit will be. If, for example, you want to cut down on sugary drinks, you could start by replacing one drink a day with a glass of water.

And in another example, instead of reaching for an unhealthy snack or chewing your nails when you're stressed or anxious, you might learn and practise a simple breathing exercise, take a short walk, talk with someone else about what you're stressed or anxious about. Instead of biting your nails, you could try massaging your hands or chewing gum. You might not be able to eliminate the cue – stress and anxiety – but you can pair it with a more positive behaviour.

What is a habit you'd like to change? What positive replacement habit could you do instead? Try different replacement behaviours and see what works for you.

Use visualisation

Picture the situation and mentally rehearse carrying out the replacement behaviour.

For example, suppose you're trying to break the habit of ordering chips with every meal. You know you're going out for dinner at the weekend and want to choose a salad instead. Take a moment beforehand to visualise yourself looking at the menu (if the restaurant provides the menu on its website, look at it in advance). Imagine feeling the urge to order chips – and then choosing the salad instead.

And in another example, if you want to drink less alcohol at a party where you know you'll be offered another drink, picture yourself being offered another drink and then asking for a soft drink or saying, 'I'm fine for now, thanks', and immediately turning back to conversation you were having.

By mentally practising the replacement behaviour your brain recognises the cue and is prepared to choose the better option when the real moment arrives. It's done it before, so it can do it again.

Change your identity

Bad habits become even stronger when your self-image supports them. For example, if you tell yourself and others, 'I often stay up too late watching rubbish TV – it's a habit,

I can't help it', you're more likely to do exactly that: stay up too late watching rubbish TV. The belief becomes self-fulfilling, and your behaviour matches the story you're telling yourself.

On page 160 you were asked to consider what you tell yourself and other people about a bad habit that you have.

Just as you can replace a bad habit with a good one, you can replace an unhelpful identity with a positive, supportive one. All the guidance in Chapter 8 about creating a positive identity applies here too. The process is the same: decide who you want to become, take a first small step towards becoming that person, and then reinforce that new identity through your actions and the way you talk about yourself.

As you consistently behave differently, you build evidence for yourself that this is who you are becoming. Over time, that evidence strengthens both the identity and the behaviour that supports it.

In many cases, you don't even need to create a new identity – you can simply return to a positive one you already had.

Try framing the change as a return to someone you once were – someone who, at some point in the past, was, for example, a non-smoker or someone who didn't vape or didn't spend all evening on their phone. This perspective helps your 'new' identity feel familiar and attainable – something that fits naturally with who you know you're capable of being.

Lasting change is more likely when a new behaviour aligns with your identity – your sense of who you are. Remember: you become what you repeatedly think and do.

Make a fresh start

You can choose to start a change in behaviour at any time, but research (see pages 46–47) shows that 'temporal landmarks' – meaningful dates that mark a new beginning, such as the start of the week, month, or year, a birthday, or returning from a holiday – do give you a motivational advantage. These moments can act as a mental reset button, creating a psychological separation between your 'old self' and your 'new self'. The separation between the two states helps boosts optimism – you feel like you're starting from a clean slate – which increases motivation.

Using a temporal landmark to kick-start a behaviour change doesn't guarantee success, but it can create emotional momentum, making the decision to start feel more meaningful and motivating.

Focus on the 'new you': if you do slip up for some reason, don't see it as having failed – don't berate yourself. Instead, see it a mistake made by the 'old you' and move back to the path the 'new you' is taking.

Get support from others

Let family, friends, and colleagues know what you're aiming for. It's easier to break a habit when those around you support the change. When others ask about your progress and encourage you or share their experience, you don't feel so alone in your efforts.

Look for others who have managed to break a bad habit – people who have made a change for the better. Talk to them about it. Ask the following.

- How and why did you decide to stop the bad habit?
- What new behaviour (if any) did you replace it with?
- What would you recommend as the easiest first step?
- Have you slipped up at any point? What happened?
- How did you get back on track?

Learning about their specific strategies and how they manage any difficulties gives you guidance and ideas that you can use to start making a change in your own behaviour.

Track progress. Acknowledge and celebrate small wins

Tracking your progress boosts motivation. As you see change – even small changes – you build confidence in your ability to control or reduce the behaviour.

Keep a simple record by writing down how often you resisted an urge and avoided the bad habit. Make a mark too for each time you perform the replacement habit.

Tracking your change in behaviour makes progress visible and can help you see that you are becoming the person you want to be. A paper-based daily habit tracker – a diary or calendar or a habit tracker app – can help you keep a record.

If you slip back into the bad habit for any length of time, it's important that you don't berate yourself and give up. (More on this in Chapter 9.)

Most importantly, be aware of small wins. If, for example, you successfully avoided screens for the first hour of your day, acknowledge it. No matter that it was only for the first hour of the day, it's a step in the right direction.

Do give yourself a treat each time you reach a milestone – go to Chapter 7 and read about tiered rewards for more information on this.

Top tip

Surf the urge
Anytime you feel yourself tempted to break your good intentions and slip into a bad habit, surf the urge. Imagine the urge to slip back into a habit as a wave in the ocean. It will build in intensity, but soon break and disappear.

Breathe. Pause and focus on your breathing for just one minute. Then imagine yourself riding the wave, not fighting it, but also not giving into it. Know that cravings aren't permanent, they come – and then they go. Just like the waves.

Be kind

Any time you slip back into a bad habit, don't berate yourself. Criticising yourself only makes change harder, not easier. Feeling bad about a mistake increases stress – and stress often triggers the very habit you're trying to break.

When you feel guilty or frustrated, your motivation drops. It's easy to think you've 'ruined everything', which can lead to giving up altogether. But a setback doesn't erase your progress, and it doesn't have to hinder your progress.

Slips are a normal part of the process; they're not signs of failure but simply signs that you're still rewiring your behaviour. (All the information in Chapter 9 – Six steps to change, Beginner's mind, Use the word 'but', and The million-dollar question – can help you here.)

Any time you slip up, the most helpful response is to pause and reflect on what happened: what triggered the behaviour? What could you do differently next time?

Treating yourself with kindness and patience helps you reset more quickly and supports the positive identity you're on your way to achieving.

Key points

Self-awareness

- Understanding how bad habits are formed and established is the first step to breaking them. The next step is to identify the cues, triggers, and context; the routine, rewards, and identity associated with a habit you want to break.
- Ask yourself why breaking a particular habit matters to you. Think about what the habit is costing you, what you'll gain, and how it connects to the person you want to become. This reframes habit change as an act of self-care rather than one of discipline or punishment.

Positive thinking

- When you think about changing a habit in terms of what you want to gain rather than what you want to avoid, you create a more sustainable approach. It feels optimistic and empowering, not restrictive or punishing, and your mind becomes more willing to accept and move toward the change.

Small steps

- Trying to quit a habit in one go can feel overwhelming. In contrast, taking small, gradual steps makes breaking a bad habit more manageable – it requires less self-discipline and willpower, which makes it more likely that you'll start and keep going.
- Each small success strengthens your belief that you *can* change.
- Small steps allow for easier adjustments. If something isn't working, rather than feel you've failed, you can easily adjust your approach based on what you've learned.
- Changing a habit slowly but steadily helps build and strengthen new neural pathways, which makes it much more likely that you'll stick with the new behaviour over the long term.
- All it takes is a little effort at the start. Start with that first step and keep moving forward. You'll gain momentum and it's easier to continue doing it.
- Still hesitating? Then make the step even smaller. Try and work out what would be the smallest version – one that would move you in the right direction.

Get prepared

- It could be that preparation is your first step. Preparing to stop a habit means setting the conditions for change before trying to change the behaviour itself.
- Preparation is one of the six stages of change. Even though you haven't begun to break the habit yet, preparation still counts as progress.

Change your environment

- By deliberately organising the spaces in your home, you can make supportive habits easier. Doing this also acts as a preparatory step.
- When a place becomes associated with a habit, the environment does the reminding for you. That reduces reliance on willpower and helps good habits become easier while making unwanted habits less automatic.

Make it harder to do

- Out of sight really can mean out of mind. When you make a cue less visible or less convenient, you make it far less likely that you'll be prompted to repeat the habit. So, to weaken a habit loop, remove the associated cues and triggers.

Replace the habit

- When you stop a habit, you create an empty space in the habit loop. If the cue is still present, your brain expects something to happen. A replacement behaviour fills that gap in the loop – the cue and reward remain, but the habit has changed to a more positive behaviour.

Use visualisation

- By mentally practising the replacement behaviour, your brain recognises the cue and is prepared to choose the better option when the real moment arrives. It's done it before, so it can do it again.

Change your identity

- Replace an unhelpful identity with a positive, supportive one. Decide who you want to become and take a first small step towards eliminating the bad habit and becoming that person. Reinforce that new identity by the way you talk about yourself.
- As you consistently behave differently, you build evidence for yourself that this is who you are becoming. Over time, that evidence strengthens both the identity and the behaviour that supports it.
- In many cases, you don't need to create a new identity – you can reconnect with a positive one you already had. Framing the change as a return to who you once were makes the identity feel familiar, realistic, and aligned with who you know you're capable of being.

Make a fresh start

- You can use the 'fresh start effect' to kick-start a change in behaviour by using a temporal landmark, such as the start of a week, month, or year, a birthday, an anniversary, or after returning from a holiday.
- Focus on the 'new you'. If you do slip up don't berate yourself. See it as a mistake made by the 'old you' and return to the path the 'new you' is taking.

Get support from others

- Let family, friends, and colleagues know what you're aiming for. It's easier to break a habit when those around you support the change. When others ask about your progress, and encourage you or share their experience, you don't feel so alone in your efforts.
- Look for others who have managed to break a bad habit – people who have made a change for the better. Talk to them about it. Learning about their specific strategies and how they managed any difficulties gives you guidance and ideas that you can use to start making a change in your own behaviour.

Track progress

- Tracking your change in behaviour – using a diary, calendar, or habit app – makes progress visible and can help you see that you are becoming the person you want to be.
- Be aware of small wins – no matter how small, a win is a step in the right direction. When you reach milestones, such as a week or a month without the habit, give yourself a specific reward to reinforce your progress.

Surf the urge

- Anytime you're tempted to slip back into a bad habit, surf the urge. Imagine the urge as a wave in the ocean. It will build in intensity, but soon break and disappear.

Be kind

- If you do slip back into a bad habit, don't berate yourself. Feeling bad about a mistake increases stress – and stress often triggers the very habit you're trying to break.

- The most helpful response is to reflect on what happened: what triggered the behaviour? What could you do differently next time?
- Treating yourself with kindness and patience helps you reset more quickly and supports the positive identity you're on your way to achieving.

12
Habits, Addictions, and Obsessive-Compulsive Disorder

The UK's National Health Service defines addiction as 'not having control over doing, taking or using something to the point where it could be harmful to you' (nhs.uk/live-well/addiction-support/addiction-what-is-it).

A person can have conscious control over a habit, but an addiction is a compulsive need that is not easily stopped, even when the person is aware of harmful consequences. The behaviour controls them, leading to a feeling of powerlessness.

The rehab facility Acquiesce Rehab (acquiesce.org.uk) state that 'Addiction is much more complex than a habit due to the way in which it can change the brain's structure and function, rewiring the reward circuit and leading to intense cravings. This makes it a chronic disease of the brain, whereas a habit is an automatic response of the brain which can be unlearned'.

Addiction is most commonly associated with substances such as drugs, alcohol, and smoking and behaviours such as gambling. 'But', say the NHS 'it's possible to be addicted to just about anything, including work, internet, solvents, shopping and sex'.

The NHS explains that: 'being addicted to something means that not having it causes withdrawal symptoms, or a "come down". Because this can be unpleasant, it's easier to carry on having or doing what you crave, and so the cycle continues. Often, an addiction gets out of control because you need more and more to satisfy a craving and achieve the "high".

The strain of managing an addiction can seriously damage your work life and relationships. In the case of substance misuse (for example, drugs and alcohol), an addiction can have serious psychological and physical effects'.

If you have a habit that for you is just something that you find annoying – but has very little to no negative effects on your life – then it is simply a habit. However, when a habit becomes damaging and has serious negative consequences on your relationships, job, health, and finances, then it is likely an addiction.

The steps described in Chapter 11 can help you break a bad habit before it turns into an addiction. If, though, you're concerned that your habit may have become an addiction, you can get help.

The NHS says that 'Addiction is a treatable condition. You could see your GP for advice or contact an organisation that specialises in helping people with addictions'. The NHS suggests the following online directories to find addiction treatment services in your area:

- www.nhs.uk/nhs-services/find-alcohol-addiction-support-services
- www.nhs.uk/service-search/other-health-services/drug-addiction-support
- www.nhs.uk/service-search/other-health-services/smoking-cessation-clinic

To speak to someone anonymously about any type of addiction, you can call the Samaritans (www.samaritans.org) on 116–123.

Habits and OCD

Obsessive-Compulsive Disorder (OCD)

Obsessive-Compulsive Disorder (OCD) is an anxiety-related condition where a person experiences frequent intrusive, obsessive thoughts and compulsive behaviour.

The obsessive part of OCD is the unpleasant, persistent, and uncontrollable thought, image, worry or fear, impulse or urge that repeatedly enters the mind. These thoughts, worries, etc., can cause feelings of unease, distress, anxiety, or disgust.

The compulsive part of OCD is the repetitive behaviour or mental thought rituals that a person feels they need to carry out over and over again in an attempt to relieve the anxiety caused by the obsessive thoughts. Examples of compulsions are excessive cleaning, checking, counting, measuring, ordering, and repeating tasks or actions. But OCD presents itself in many guises, not just hand washing or checking locks or light switches.

Once the compulsion has been carried out, the anxiety lessens. It is, though, possible to experience obsessive thoughts only and not feel the need to carry out a compulsion.

The unwanted, intrusive, disturbing thoughts significantly interfere with day-to-day life as they are very difficult to ignore. Someone with OCD may realise that their obsessional thoughts are irrational but feel that the only way to relieve the anxiety caused by these thoughts is to perform compulsive behaviours, often to prevent perceived harm happening to themselves or to a loved one.

Both habits and OCD can be triggered by cues or situations that set off the behaviour. In both cases, the actions are repeated and often carried out automatically. Both OCD and habits also rely on learning and reinforcement in the brain: the behaviour continues because it reduces discomfort or provides a sense of relief.

Habits are learned routines that can be neutral, helpful, unhelpful, or harmful. They usually serve a practical or rewarding purpose and are controllable – always locking the door before bed, for example, or engaging in physical exercise – doing 10 squats or push-ups each morning or taking a walk every lunchtime.

In contrast, OCD behaviours are repetitive behaviours that a person does in order to reduce intense anxiety caused by obsessions – intrusive, distressing thoughts or fears. For example, returning to the door to check that it's locked even if they've checked it several times already.

Physical exercise can become an OCD behaviour when it's done to neutralise anxiety or prevent a feared outcome, rather than for fitness or enjoyment. For example, a person might have an intrusive thought such as 'If I don't do this exactly right, something bad will happen'. To relieve that anxiety, they might do 10 squats, but then feel it wasn't 'right' and repeat until it feels correct (even if that means 50 or more). Another example is someone who runs or walks a specific number of steps to prevent something bad from happening.

A person engaged in a healthy exercise habit is flexible, can skip exercise without fretting and panicking about it. In contrast, when a person is engaged in OCD-related physical exercise, their behaviour is rigid, urgent, anxiety-driven, and hard to stop. They *have* to do it, even when they know they're excessive or irrational.

In every case OCD behaviour temporarily relieves anxiety but reinforces the obsession, creating a distressing cycle. Habits are automatic behaviours, but they don't involve the same level of distress or impact on a person's daily life as OCD.

A person can have conscious control over a habit – a habit can be changed with awareness and effort. OCD behaviours are part of a clinical disorder that usually requires therapy such Cognitive Behavioural Therapy or Exposure and Response Prevention or medication to manage effectively.

Getting help for OCD

It's important to get help if you think you have OCD and it's having a significant impact on your life. OCD is unlikely to get better on its own, but treatment and support are available to help you manage your symptoms and have a better quality of life.

For further information go to: www.nhs.uk/mental-health/conditions/obsessive-compulsive-disorder-ocd/symptoms

Make an appointment to see your GP or refer yourself to an NHS talking therapies service to get a proper diagnosis and treatment (www.nhs.uk/nhs-services/mental-health-services/find-nhs-talking-therapies-for-anxiety-and-depression).

If you ever feel you cannot go on:

Call 111. Or 999.
Call 116 123 to talk to the Samaritans, or email: jo@samaritans
.org for a reply within 24 hours.

Key points

Habits and addictions

- A habit is an automatic behaviour that you can consciously control, while an addiction is a compulsive need that continues despite harmful consequences and often leads to feelings of powerlessness.
- Addiction is more complex than a habit because it alters brain structure and function, rewiring the reward system and creating intense cravings, making it a chronic brain condition rather than a learned behaviour.
- Addictions are commonly linked to substances like drugs, alcohol, and nicotine, but can also involve behaviours such as gambling, work, internet use, shopping, or sex.
- Addiction involves withdrawal symptoms and increasing tolerance, meaning more of the substance or behaviour is needed to achieve the same effect, which keeps the cycle going.
- When a behaviour causes serious harm to health, relationships, work, or finances, it is likely an addiction rather than a relatively harmless or annoying habit.

Habits and Obsessive-Compulsive Disorder (OCD)

- Obsessive-Compulsive Disorder (OCD) is an anxiety-related condition involving intrusive, distressing thoughts (obsessions) and repetitive behaviours or mental rituals (compulsions) performed to relieve anxiety.
- Compulsions – such as checking, cleaning, counting, or repeating actions – temporarily reduce anxiety, even though the person may recognise the thoughts as irrational; OCD can also involve obsessions without visible compulsions.
- Like habits, OCD behaviours can be triggered by cues and reinforced through relief, but in OCD the intrusive thoughts and compulsions significantly interfere with daily life and are difficult to control.
- Habits are learned routines that can be helpful, neutral, or unhelpful, are usually flexible and purposeful (e.g., exercising for health), and can be changed with awareness and effort.
- OCD behaviours are repetitive actions driven by intrusive, distressing thoughts and performed to reduce intense anxiety or prevent feared outcomes (e.g., repeated checking or rigid exercise rituals).
- Unlike habits, OCD behaviours are urgent, anxiety-driven, and hard to stop, temporarily relieving distress while reinforcing the obsession, and typically require clinical treatment such as CBT, ERP, or medication.

Good Habit Action Plan

*The habit

What is the new habit? Why do you want to start doing it?

The habit is: _____

I want to start doing it because _____

*Support from others

Who can support you with your new habit? How will they support you? It might be a friend, family member, or a community that shares the same interest.

I will get support from _____

I'll ask them to _____

*The smallest step

What will be your first small step?

My first small step will be _____

*Implementation intention

When, where, and how will you do it?

Example: On Monday, Wednesday, and Friday at 7 a.m. in the living room, I'll join an online exercise class.

When _____ Where _____

I will (habit)_____

*Habit chain

Do you have a habit or routine that you will attach the new one to?

After or before (current habit)_____ I will (new habit)_____

*Your environment

How can you arrange your environment to remind you – to make it easier to do the habit?

Example: at night, I'll put my phone on a table across the room and put a book on my bed.

I will put/place _____

in/at _____

so I'm reminded to _____

*Enjoyment and rewards

What, if anything, will you do to help you enjoy the new habit? What will you immediately reward the habit with? How, if at all, might you vary the enjoyment and rewards?

While I do the habit, I will: _____

After I do the habit, I will: _____

I'll vary the enjoyment and/or reward by _____

*Track your progress

What's a simple way to track your progress?

I'll track it by: ☐ calendar ☐ notebook ☐ app ☐ other: _____

*Slip ups

What will you tell yourself if you break the habit for a period of time?

I didn't _____ But I can _____

*Identity shift

Who are you becoming by doing this habit?

For example: I'm becoming someone who regularly reads in the evening.

'I'm becoming someone who _____'.

Choose one new habit and complete the habit plan.

Focus on just one habit at a time and give yourself time to practise. Reflect regularly on what's working and what isn't. When it begins to feel easier, more natural, and a part of who you are, you'll be ready to move on to the next one.

Good Habit Action Plan

*The habit

What is the new habit? Why do you want to start doing it?

The habit is: _____

I want to start doing it because _____

*Support from others

Who can support you with your new habit? How will they support you? It might be a friend, family member, or a community that shares the same interest.

I will get support from _____

I'll ask them to _____

*The smallest step

What will be your first small step?

My first small step will be _____

*Implementation intention

When, where, and how will you do it?

Example: On Monday, Wednesday, and Friday at 7 a.m. in the living room, I'll join an online exercise class.

When _____ Where _____

I will (habit)_____

*Habit chain

Do you have a habit or routine that you will attach the new one to?

After or before (current habit)_____ I will (new habit)_____

*Your environment

How can you arrange your environment to remind you – to make it easier to do the habit?

Example: at night, I'll put my phone on a table across the room and put a book on my bed.

I will put/place _____

in/at _____

so I'm reminded to _____

*Enjoyment and rewards

What, if anything, will you do to help you enjoy the new habit? What will you immediately reward the habit with? How, if at all, might you vary the enjoyment and rewards?

While I do the habit, I will: _____

After I do the habit, I will: _____

I'll vary the enjoyment and/or reward by _____

*Track your progress

What's a simple way to track your progress?

I'll track it by: ☐ calendar ☐ notebook ☐ app ☐ other: _____

*Slip ups

What will you tell yourself if you break the habit for a period of time?

I didn't _____ But I can _____

*Identity shift

Who are you becoming by doing this habit?

For example: I'm becoming someone who regularly reads in the evening.

'I'm becoming someone who _____'.

Choose one new habit and complete the habit plan.

Focus on just one habit at a time and give yourself time to practise. Reflect regularly on what's working and what isn't. When it begins to feel easier, more natural, and a part of who you are, you'll be ready to move on to the next one.

Good Habit Action Plan

*The habit

What is the new habit? Why do you want to start doing it?

The habit is: _____

I want to start doing it because _____

*Support from others

Who can support you with your new habit? How will they support you? It might be a friend, family member, or a community that shares the same interest.

I will get support from _____

I'll ask them to _____

*The smallest step

What will be your first small step?

My first small step will be _____

*Implementation intention

When, where, and how will you do it?

Example: On Monday, Wednesday, and Friday at 7 a.m. in the living room, I'll join an online exercise class.

When _____ Where _____

I will (habit)_____

*Habit chain

Do you have a habit or routine that you will attach the new one to?

After or before (current habit)_____ I will (new habit)_____

*Your environment

How can you arrange your environment to remind you – to make it easier to do the habit?

Example: at night, I'll put my phone on a table across the room and put a book on my bed.

I will put/place _____

in/at _____

so I'm reminded to _____

*Enjoyment and rewards

What, if anything, will you do to help you enjoy the new habit? What will you immediately reward the habit with? How, if at all, might you vary the enjoyment and rewards?

While I do the habit, I will: _____

After I do the habit, I will: _____

I'll vary the enjoyment and/or reward by _____

*Track your progress

What's a simple way to track your progress?

I'll track it by: ☐ calendar ☐ notebook ☐ app ☐ other: _____

*Slip ups

What will you tell yourself if you break the habit for a period of time?

I didn't _____ But I can _____

*Identity shift

Who are you becoming by doing this habit?

For example: I'm becoming someone who regularly reads in the evening.

'I'm becoming someone who _____'.

Choose one new habit and complete the habit plan.

Focus on just one habit at a time and give yourself time to practise. Reflect regularly on what's working and what isn't. When it begins to feel easier, more natural, and a part of who you are, you'll be ready to move on to the next one.

Action Plan to Break a Bad Habit

*The habit

What is the habit you want to change?

The habit is: _____

*Why this change matters

What is this habit currently costing you? Why do you want to break the habit?

For example, the habit could be costing you time, energy, health, or money.

It's costing me _____

I want to break the habit because _____

*Cues, contexts, and rewards

What cues or triggers the habit?

The cue is_____

When and where does the habit usually occur?

It usually happens (when) _____ (where)
_____

What's the reward? (relief, comfort, pleasure?)

The reward is _____

*A replacement behaviour

What will be more helpful behaviour that meets the same need or reward?

A replacement behaviour will be_____

*The smallest step

What will be your first small step?

My first small step will be _____

*Your environment

How can you arrange your environment to remind you – to make it harder to do the old habit and easier to do the replacement habit?

Example. I won't buy biscuits and chocolate. I'll buy or prepare healthy snacks.

Cues or prompts I'll remove: _____

Cues or prompts I'll put in place for the new habit
_____

*Support from others

Who can support you? (It might be a friend, family member, or a community.) How will they support you?

I will get support from _____

I'll ask them to _____

*Rewards

How will you reward yourself for each milestone you reach – each week or month you consistently stick with the habit change?

I'll reward myself with _____

*Track your progress

What's a simple way to track your progress?

I'll track it by: ☐ calendar ☐ notebook ☐ app ☐ other:
_____

*Identity shift

Who are you becoming?

I am becoming someone who, instead of (old habit) _____ is now becoming someone who (new habit) _____.

*Slip ups and mistakes

What will you tell yourself if you revert back to the old habit for a period of time?

I will remind myself: 'I didn't _____, but I can _____'.

Focus on breaking one habit at a time and give yourself time to practise replacement habits. Reflect regularly on what's helping and what isn't and adjust as needed. When the old habit has lost its pull and your new behaviour feels easier and more natural, if you have another habit you want to break, you'll be ready to move onto the next one.

Action Plan to Break a Bad Habit

*The habit

What is the habit you want to change?

The habit is: _____

*Why this change matters

What is this habit currently costing you? Why do you want to break the habit?

For example, the habit could be costing you time, energy, health, or money.

It's costing me _____

I want to break the habit because _____

*Cues, contexts, and rewards

What cues or triggers the habit?

The cue is_____

When and where does the habit usually occur?

It usually happens (when) _____ (where)
_____

What's the reward? (relief, comfort, pleasure?)

The reward is _____

*A replacement behaviour

What will be more helpful behaviour that meets the same need or reward?

A replacement behaviour will be_____

*The smallest step

What will be your first small step?

My first small step will be _____

*Your environment

How can you arrange your environment to remind you – to make it harder to do the old habit and easier to do the replacement habit?

Example. I won't buy biscuits and chocolate. I'll buy or prepare healthy snacks.

Cues or prompts I'll remove: _____

Cues or prompts I'll put in place for the new habit
_____

*Support from others

Who can support you? (It might be a friend, family member, or a community.) How will they support you?

I will get support from _____

I'll ask them to _____

*Rewards

How will you reward yourself for each milestone you reach – each week or month you consistently stick with the habit change?

I'll reward myself with _____

*Track your progress

What's a simple way to track your progress?

I'll track it by: ☐ calendar ☐ notebook ☐ app ☐ other:
_____

*Identity shift

Who are you becoming?

I am becoming someone who, instead of (old habit) _____ is now becoming someone who (new habit) _____.

*Slip ups and mistakes

What will you tell yourself if you revert back to the old habit for a period of time?

I will remind myself: 'I didn't _____, but I can _____'.

Focus on breaking one habit at a time and give yourself time to practise replacement habits. Reflect regularly on what's helping and what isn't and adjust as needed. When the old habit has lost its pull and your new behaviour feels easier and more natural, if you have another habit you want to break, you'll be ready to move onto the next one.

Action Plan to Break a Bad Habit

*The habit

What is the habit you want to change?

The habit is: _____

*Why this change matters

What is this habit currently costing you? Why do you want to break the habit?

For example, the habit could be costing you time, energy, health, or money.

It's costing me _____

I want to break the habit because _____

*Cues, contexts, and rewards

What cues or triggers the habit?

The cue is_____

When and where does the habit usually occur?

It usually happens (when) _____ (where)

_____

What's the reward? (relief, comfort, pleasure?)

The reward is _____

*A replacement behaviour

What will be more helpful behaviour that meets the same need or reward?

A replacement behaviour will be_____

*The smallest step

What will be your first small step?

My first small step will be _____

*Your environment

How can you arrange your environment to remind you – to make it harder to do the old habit and easier to do the replacement habit?

Example. I won't buy biscuits and chocolate. I'll buy or prepare healthy snacks.

Cues or prompts I'll remove: _____

Cues or prompts I'll put in place for the new habit
_____

*Support from others

Who can support you? (It might be a friend, family member, or a community.) How will they support you?

I will get support from _____

I'll ask them to _____

*Rewards

How will you reward yourself for each milestone you reach – each week or month you consistently stick with the habit change?

I'll reward myself with _____

*Track your progress

What's a simple way to track your progress?

I'll track it by: ☐ calendar ☐ notebook ☐ app ☐ other:
_____

*Identity shift

Who are you becoming?

I am becoming someone who, instead of (old habit) _____ is now becoming someone who (new habit) _____.

*Slip ups and mistakes

What will you tell yourself if you revert back to the old habit for a period of time?

I will remind myself: 'I didn't _____, but I can _____'.

Focus on breaking one habit at a time and give yourself time to practise replacement habits. Reflect regularly on what's helping and what isn't and adjust as needed. When the old habit has lost its pull and your new behaviour feels easier and more natural, if you have another habit you want to break, you'll be ready to move onto the next one.

Index